NUM. 6:24-26
EPH. 3:20

THE BLACK BAPTIST CHURCH:

ITS HISTORICAL AND THEOLOGICAL PERSPECTIVE

JOSEPH MORGAN

This book is a work of non-fiction. Names of people and places have been changed to protect their privacy

© 2004 Joseph Morgan. All rights reserved.

No part of this book may be reproduced, stored in a retrieval system, or transmitted by any means, electronic, mechanical, photocopying, recording, or otherwise, without written permission from the author.

ISBN: 1-4140-3208-0 (e-book)
ISBN: 1-4140-3207-2 (Paperback)

Library of Congress Control Number: 2004090203

This book is printed on acid free paper.
Printed in the United States of America
Bloomington, IN

1stBooks – rev. 01/20/04

A Major Writing Project
Submitted to the Graduate Council
Of the
Luther Rice Seminary

In Partial Fulfillment
Of the Requirements for the Degree
Doctor of Ministry

Joseph Morgan
B.A., Saint Louis Christian College, 1971
M..R.E., Covenant Theological Seminary, 1972
May 1981

MAJOR WRITING PROJECT
APPROVAL SHEET

Candidate: Joseph Morgan

Degree: Doctor of Ministry

Title of Composition: THE BLACK BAPTIST CHURCH: ITS HISTORICAL AND THEOLOGICAL PERSPECTIVE

Purpose of Composition: The purpose of this composition is to provide information on the black Baptist church in America.

WRITING PROJECT COMMITTEE

Dr. Wesley V. Forbes
Graduate Advisor

Dr. Jerry Simpson
Dr. Saul S. Ervin

May 4, 1981
Date Approved

ACKNOWLEDGEMENTS

It is most gratifying, and very pleasing to acknowledge the amazing help of my loving, and beloved daughter, Cheryl Morgan Young, who is a computer expert, and has given me expert assistance, and is also co-author of this work. In addition to being dedicated to my daughter, Cheryl M. Young, the co-author; it is also dedicated in loving memory to my beloved wife who is at rest in the Bosom of the Lord my God. Dr. Evelyn D. Hardy Morgan served the Jerusalem Missionary Baptist Church for many years as musician, and Minister of Music During the pastorate of the late Rev. L. Q. Laws, Rev. J. A. Morgan, my father, who also served J.M.B.C. as pastor for 18 years, and my mother was First Lady during that time. So this work is also dedicated to my family members who are at rest in the Bosom of the Lord; they include my Uncle and Aunt James and Virgie Lee Myers, Sullivan and Eula Hardy, my father-in law and mother-in-law.

Dr. E. D. Hardy Morgan also served J. M. B. C. during my own pastorate as well; we formed a Ministry Team, serving not only this church of Christ at Jerusalem M. B. C., but also our Antioch District Association, the Missionary Baptist State Convention of Missouri, in the Congress of Christian Education of our State as team-teachers, and also the National Baptist Convention, USA., Inc., and National Baptist Congress of Christian Education.

Having answered the call of God to the Gospel Ministry, I preached my trial sermon here at Jerusalem, was licensed and ordained by Jerusalem M. B. Church during and under the pastorate of the late Rev. James Andrew Morgan, my dad. And, at his demise on Dec. 7, 1964, I was chosen to become his successor on March 8, 1965. My first college and seminary training was financed by the G. I. Bill until it expired; afterwards all my Ministry Education and training was taken care of by this church. Thus, serving as pastor/teacher of J.M.B.C., I must give my best in service, and pass on to this congregation that which God gives me by the anointing of His Spirit. This work is also dedicated, with love, honor, and respect, to the JERUSALEM MISSIONARY BAPTIST CHURCH OF CHRIST, my Church-Home which I serve to the best of my ability, all the people of God who worship and work in God' Kingdom here.

PREFACE

"TheBlack Baptist Church; Its Historical and Theological Perspective," was begun as a MAJOR WRITING PROJECT, in partial fulfillment of the requirements for the degree, Doctor of Ministry. That, having been completed, and the Degree earned, it became my purpose to revise this work for publication. There is a publication available today entitled "How The Bible Came To Be," that tells much about how we got our Bible. The Key Resource, Producer, and Author, is God Himself through, and by the work of the Holy Spirit. What we know of God, is what God Himself has told us in His Book, The Holy Bible. The Word of God was not given so that we may learn and know something ABOUT GOD, but so that we may **KNOW GOD HIMSELF; SO THAT WE MAY KNOW THE TRUTH,** and just as JESUS TAUGHT**, THE TRUTH WILL MAKE YOU FREE.** In our world today, there are so many young black people who have not been taught anything at all about the history of the black race, and very little, if anything, about the black church; especially the **BLACK BAPTIST CHURCH.**

It is my hope that this book will inspire our young people to seek to learn more **of who we are, and where we came from and how we got here, through the Middle Passaage, to America; and that they will be inspired to seek a greater knowledge of God, in and through the black Baptist church; that they may learn who we are, and <u>Whose we are.</u>**

Now as a published work I hope that many of our people, both young and older adults will discover the paths over which our race has trod to get to where we are now, and will be inspired to continue the upward ascent in the paths of life on the Highway to heaven, so that what we do, how we act, our conversation, our walk, and our lifestyle will always be a source of aspiration and inspiration in the lives of those with whom we associate to the glory of God our Father through Jesus Christ our Lord. And, as the Apostle Paul states in Philippians 3:8 ff., ". . . I count all things but loss for the excellency of the knowledge of Christ Jesus my Lord . . . that I may win Christ. And be found in Him, not having my own righteousness, which is of the law, but that which is through the faith of Christ, the righteousness which is of God by faith: that I might know Him, and the power of His resurrection, and the fellowship of His sufferings, being made conformable unto His death; if by any means I might attain unto the resurrection of the dead. And, to God be the glory for all the things He has done.

Joseph Morgan

Table of Contents

ACKNOWLEDGEMENTS	vii
PREFACE	xi
INTRODUCTION	xix
P A R T O N E	1
THE BLACK BAPTIST CHURCH	1
IN HISTORICAL PERSPECTIVE	1
Chapter I	2
A BACKGROUND OF SLAVERY	2
Roots in Africa	10
Sold into Slavery	13
From Africa to America	19
Chapter 2	24
THE LOSS OF IDENTITY	24
The Loss of Name and Personality	25
The Loss of Family, Tribe, and Friends	27
The Loss of Human Rights	32
The Subjugation of the Individual Will	34
The Duration of Slavery	37
Chapter 3	48
THE PERIOD OF TRANSITION	48
Slaves Searching for the God of Love	54
Streaks of Light In Chains of Darkness	57
Slaves and Slaveholders in the Same Church	60
Service	61
Church Services for Slaves	64
The Great Dilemma	67

Chapter 4	**71**
THE END OF AN ERA	71
The Desire To Be Free	73
Slave Uprisings	75
Abolitionist Movements	77
The First Black Baptist Church	78
The Emancipation Proclamation	86
Reconstruction, Constitutional Amendments, and The Bill of Rights	96
PART TWO	**102**
THE BLACK BAPTIST CHURCH	102
I N THEOLOGICAL PERSPECTIVE	102
Chapter 5	**103**
RELIGIOUS LIFE ON THE PLANTATIONS	103
Preaching On The Plantations	106
Religious Teaching On The Plantations	109
Colored Churches On The Plantations	112
Emerging Problems of Colored Churches on The Plantations	115
Colored Baptist Churches In Urban Areas	118
Chapter 6	124
ASSOCIATIONS OF "COLORED" BAPTIST CHURCHES	124
Sharing Common Experiences	127
Sharing Learning Experiences	131
Sharing in Community Revivals	134
Sharing In Missionary Emphasis	137

Chapter 7 **141**
COLORED BAPTIST CONVENTIONS 141
Missionary and Education Conventions 143
Regional Conventions 146
State Conventions 146
National Organizations 149
Growing Pains 166

INTRODUCTION

The study of the black Baptist church has been undertaken to provide informational background and insight into the historical and theological perspective that moves the black Baptist and gives motivation for his actions. While the present work is by no means intended as an in-depth, extensive study of the black Baptist church, it could become the basis for a closer look at religion in the black community, its successes and failures, and the rise of black cults. It may also suggest some means as to how the Christian church may deal with the practice in the community within the shadow of the church.

The black Baptist church has acquired its denominational identity from the white Baptist church generally, and the Southern Baptist church in particular. The doctrinal practices of the two bodies are basically parallel; baptism by immersion in water upon a profession of faith in Jesus the Christ, thereby gaining entrance into the church, the Body of Christ, and admission to the Lord's Table. The local church is autonomous in its' own affairs; and, the New Testament in particular, and the Bible, the Word of God is its'<u>only and</u>

sufficient rule for faith and practice. This is Baptist polity and practice. Our doctrinal beliefs are alike, arising solely from Scripture, the divine revelation of God in Jesus Christ the Only Begotten, the Incarnate, and virgin-born Son of God, born of the Virgin Mary. She was espoused to Joseph the carpenter, of the house and lineage of David the king. His life and teachings are the only Standards for Christian living. His sufferings and death are the supreme sacrifice and atonement for sins. His victory is our victory, through His death, burial, and resurrection; His ascension into glory, from whence He shall return as the Righteous Judge. By virtue of our faith in the merits of that saving work of Christ as the only and just penalty for our sins, we shall live and reign with Him at His return. By His death He atoned for our sins, and by His living He secures salvation for us believers, and our lives are hid with God in Him. The articles of faith setting forth our system of beliefs, and the Baptist Church Covenant are all derived from the white Baptist Family. These same tenets of faith are also adopted by the black Baptist Family. There is one important difference in the two Families that determine the perspective of each, and that is race-experience and background.

Logically, the minister, as a seminarian, is taught that the sermon preparation must be based, at least in part, upon the needs of the congregation. The black preacher, therefore, must deal with issues, circumstances, and conditions that confront the black Christian on a daily basis, or he will discover that his preaching is foreign to his congregation. He must be able to express Biblical principles in the language of his people. The writer's own concept of "Black Theology," while it may differ from the professional, militant norm, does however, get to the sense of the general thought raised by the expression, and that is to express the truth of the gospel in terms that the man in the pew may understand, and then to apply that truth within the context of his daily life experience. In a word, expressing theological truths from the Bible in such a way that the gospel of Christ transcends both racial and cultural limitations to bring the hearer to a living, personal experience with God on a daily basis.

PART ONE

THE BLACK BAPTIST CHURCH IN HISTORICAL PERSPECTIVE

Chapter I

A BACKGROUND OF SLAVERY

The black Baptist church in the United States of America had its conception and birth when slavery was the law of the land. The primary objective of slavery was the subjugation of the black African people who were brought to this country in chains for sale at auctions to the highest bidder. The practice of slavery in this country has had many far-reaching effects upon thousands, even millions of people in America, both black and white. Although the general practice of slavery as an institution is no longer, the ugly scars which it left behind cannot be erased. Many treatises have been written on the subject of slavery, but the historical

The Black Baptist Church

record remains incomplete. Authors have treated different aspects of the subject-matter; historians have set down what could be gathered from available documents, tax records, sales contracts, ships' cargo manifests, plantation papers, etc,. but the practice of slavery was so widespread, and varied from area to area that any attempt to exhaust the subject could prove to be an exercise in futility. Yet, from what has been written, one may easily grasp the general tenor of conditions under which the slaves were held for so many years.

While hundreds of thousands of others have come to America for many and varied reasons; the pursuit of ideals, science and navigational skills, discoveries, wealth, freedom of religion, etc.; the black African /the Negro, was brought in chains. The long process of colonization of the New World was brought about in part through the importation of persecuted and outlawed Europeans as indentured laborers, and thus the prospect of something better gave rise to new hope as one neared the end of such contractual obligations. Such was not the case with the African slave; the Negro. His impressions of New World fortunes and golden opportunities were non-existent. Under the lash of the whip, the

Joseph Morgan

burden of chains, the stench of filth, and at the mercy of the merciless the Negro/the black African came from Africa as a slave in chains. The prospect of his future in America was, at best, dark and dismal; and at worst, hopelessness and disparagement. For so many generations the Negro's greatest joy was the release brought about by death. This fact is borne out by many of the songs of the slaves after years as beasts of burden. Some of those songs which were the outgrowth of long years of slavery are: "Over my Head I Hear Music in the Air," "Steal Away to Jesus," "Swing Low Sweet Chariot," "Nobody Knows de Trouble I See," "By an' By I'm gwinter lay down my heavy load," and a great many others, the listing of which, time and space will not permit.

The beginning of the slave trade in the American Colonies is said to have bgun at the Jamestown settlement in Virginia on August 20, 1619 when a Dutch vessel, a fighting ship, landed twenty black native Africans who were bought by colonial settlers almost immediately. [1]

Bergman (1969) dates the beginning of the Negro's history in America with the re-discovery of Africa by the Portuguese. Several Moors had been taken captive by a captain in the service of Henry the Navigator. These Moors

The Black Baptist Church

were of noble birth along the African coast, and to secure their release, the Moors offered as ransom, ten blacks, male and female. The ransom was accepted, and the blacks, Africans; were brought to Lisboa and sold at the market. This transaction represented the beginning of the African slave trade which, until the year 1517, was based on a Papal grant, monopolized by the Portuguese crown. Henry the Navigator sought to put an end to the abuses of the slave trade and forbade the kidnapping of Negroes in 1455. Even so, however, it continued; for in the ecclesiastical annals of Ortiz de Zuniga in 1474 Negro slaves were here in great numbers, and the tithes that were levied on them produced considerable gains in royal revenues. The first slave trading post, Port Sao Jorge de Mina, was built by the Portuguese in 1482 on the African Gold Coast.[2]

Christians in Western Europe began to turn their attention to the trade in men around the fifteenth and sixteenth centuries, but this was not the beginning of a new practice among human beings. While there was originality in their approach and technique, this pursuit had been this pursuit had been the common concern of men for numerous centuries. During the very earliest known history of Africa, slavery was widespread here as it was on other continents. It is logical to believe that there was cruelty and oppression in African slavery, just as it was anywhere the institution developed. In some areas of Africa there was no racial basis for slavery. The Egyptians enslaved whatever peoples they captured. Some were Semitic, others were Mediterraneans, and still others were blacks from Ethiopia. In both the Greek and Roman empires slavery was well known. During both periods the traffic in men brought a continuous stream of slaves to perform personal services and till the fields of the ruling class. This menial service was not considered as degrading in Greece and Rome. Opportunities for education, and cultural advancement, was therefore opened up to slaves. It was not at all unusual to find slaves with a degree of intelligence and training that was not usually associated with persons of this class.[3]

It is worthy of note that when the Mohammedans invaded Africa, they contributed greatly to the institution of Negro slavery in a number of ways. They seized the Negro women for their harems, and took Negro men for military

The Black Baptist Church

and menial service. Moslems sought Negro slaves by both pure chase, and by conquest, and shipped them off to Arabia, Persia, or some other land of Islam. Then, as Negro kings and princes embraced the Mohammedan faith, they co-operated with the Arabians in the exploitation and exporting of human cargo.

Slavery among the Mohammedans was not primarily aimed at the pursuit of wealth through the production of goods. For, in these lands, Arabia, Persia, and Egypt, there were no extensive cotton fields, tobacco plantations, or sugar cane fields to be cultivated, planted, and harvested. Slaves in these states were primarily servants, and the demand for them was in proportion to the wealth of the prospective masters. As such, it appeared that slavery was more a manifestation of wealth, rather than the pursuits of acquiring wealth. The harshness and severity of slavery in the Western hemisphere where the institution became the primary means of acquiring wealth was almost non-existent under the Mohammedans. It is noteworthy that the slaves who were converted to Islam achieved standing as brothers among their masters. They were not released from their roles as bond servants, but they were elevated in their standing among their fellow-servants. While the institution of slavery continued, this practice may have seemed to be of doubtful value; though it could have been seen by slaves of the later and more ruthless system as a desirable straw worth clinging to.[4]

Those forces released by the Renaissance the Commercial Revolution brought into existence the modern institution of slavery and the slave trade in the Western world. The Renaissance gave rise to a new kind of freedom; the freedom to pursue those ends most beneficial to one's personal interests. Those pursuits developed into such a passion-ate search that in the process, that the rights of others were, not only violated, but even destroyed. The rights of others to pursue those same ends for their own benefits were suppressed and denied. This new concept of freedom which emerged in the wake of the Renaissance bordered on the licentious and brought about a situation that approached anarchy. This was a kind of freedom which granted some the right to exploit the rights of others; a freedom that entailed little, if indeed any, social responsibility.

The Black Baptist Church

In addition to the new concept of freedom was the vital new economic life of Europe introduced by the Commercial Revolution and the prospect of grand new possibilities anticipated by the power which wealth could bring. These, taken with numerous other factors, served to unharness a base passion which fed itself on the slave trade. Thus the trade in human cargo, by Mohammedans who invaded the coasts of Africa, spreads through Arab States to Western European States, from land to land, coast to coast; the major commodity being the black skins from Africa. How ever evil the system was, it could not have gained the prominence that it did without the help of the Negroes themselves. Blacks hunted and trapped other blacks, and sold them to commercial slavers. The exploitation of the African Blacks was of such that it reduced his concept of himself to mere animal existence, non-human, and devoid of personhood and soul. He was taught to prey upon his fellow natives for a price. Not all Africans were enslaved, however; but the ones who came to the New World from Africa, whose blood and bones lay beneath the soil of this land, and their posterity, the Afro-American of today came from a background of hard, cruel slavery.

Joseph Morgan
Roots in Africa

There is something inherent in a seed or plant that distinguishes it from every other seed or plant and gives it identity as a particular class or kind. While there is a distinct difference in animate and inanimate life, there is something about the place of one's origin that plays an important role in what one becomes in life.

The captive blacks were prepared for human bondage by a process which Franklin (1967) calls "seasoning." That process was not necessarily limited to any single phase of operation. It was at least threefold in its scope. It began with chains, it was intensified through the slave codes, and finalized when the slave reached his final destination in the New World where he was considered, and treated, as an animal without a soul. He was sold at auction and became the property of others, and served as a beast of burden in the bonds of physical slavery.[5]

The science of genetics in our modern society has the same ends in view as that which was to have been accomplished through the seasoning process, to 'create' the perfect individual for a particular purpose through cloning. Or, perhaps the other extreme, the creation of a super race.

The controlling idea in seasoning was to erase the past of the captives from Africa: his family ties, tribal customs, culture, religious practices; everything that was a part of his make-up was taken away in order to fit him for his present purpose which, then, was servitude at hard labor and perfect obedience to his task-master and owner. Because of the inferior, sub-human standard assigned to slaves they were excluded from all society. Learning, the arts, religion, and culture were denied to slaves in the frontiers of the New World. But instead of achieving the stated purpose of re-orientation, ties and culture of the past were somehow reinforced. Deeply embedded in them was their African origin. People are born into a culture, and the traits of a people are characteristic of the culture from which they arise. Students of sociology have long discussed the question of whether African culture may have been transplanted and preserved in the New World. There were those who contended that Africa was void of anything approaching civilization, and

Joseph Morgan

therefore, there was nothing for the Africans to bring with them.

To be sure, there was wide dispersion of the blacks in the New World for obvious reasons. Families were separated, clans were broken up and divided in order to forestall the possibility of uprisings and insurrections. It gave assurance to the slave-owners that it would be virtually impossible for the Negroes to ever exert any influence as a group. It should be remembered, however, that the Negro slaves came from a rather complex social and economic life, and that they were not overwhelmed or overawed by conditions which they found in the New World. There were many common and shared experiences to draw them together in the fashioning of new customs and traditions that reflected their African background.

Generally, the surname assigned to a slave was an indication of whose property he, or she was. In order to be able to understand and obey the commands of the owners, the slave was required to learn the traditional vernacular—at least in the spoken form—of the New World. To know what

The Black Baptist Church

was expected of them, they had to learn the customs of their captors. These things were driven into the slaves like rusty nails into a resistive board. In addition to this there were at least two other processes of acculturation that paralleled each other in the slaves' new environment in this country: as Africans of differing experiences and backgrounds lived and worked together, there was the interaction of varying African customs that produced a different set of customs and practices which displayed roots deep in the African experiences. At the same time, there was the interaction of the African and Western cultures which, no doubt, changed the culture patterns of both groups.[6]

Prominent among those things that remained was the ability of the African to bring together two or three different and distinct beat-patterns into one harmonious rhythm, and to dance to such a rhythmic pattern without missing a step. This was uniquely African.[7]

Sold into Slavery

Slavery was not a unique institution to the Africans. The idea of slavery is about as old as the family of man. It has been the practice of peoples and nations for many centuries: <u>subjugate;</u> <u>dominate;</u> <u>enslave.</u> The classic example of slavery in the Bible was the enslavement of the Hebrews by the Egyptians. The motivating factor was given as fear. The fear expressed was that the foreigners in the land (the Hebrews, in this case) might aid or support a potential enemy of Egypt and bring the land under some foreign nation. The logical strategy of the rulers was to prevent such a possibility, so the Hebrews were enslaved as bond-servants of the Egyptians.

Through the centuries men have failed to recognize a simple truth; that one cannot enslave another without at the same time enslaving one's self. Divine retribution and the ruler-ship of God within the nations and kingdoms of men are facts which are often overlooked, if not entirely ignored. In the Biblical context, a chain of unfavorable circumstances in one man's family led ultimately to the bondage of an entire nation. Favoritism by a father for one son above other sons in the family caused jealousy and hatred with a lust for the shedding of a brother's blood; but as an alternative to bloodshed, the brothers sold their brother into slavery.

The Black Baptist Church

Peoples who have dealt in human cargo from primitive to more recent times have, in the process, become victims of their own acts. While exerting force to conquer and enslave their captives, of necessity they make themselves the bondservants of fear. Fear has driven some to very brutal means in order to preserve their ill-gotten gains.

The foundation upon which the institution of slavery rested was the desire of some to advance their own causes at the expense of others, no matter what the cost might be. Early civilization saw families and clans pursuing occupations according to the needs of their peoples. The more popular pursuits were agriculture, hunting, fishing, and livestock. The farmer's concerns with the varied occupations of farm life made him prey to the more aggressive herdsmen and hunters. When people are overrun by invaders and intruders they begin seeking some means of escape, some way to overcome their difficulties.

The African was more familiar with his own homeland than the sailors who crossed the oceans and seas in search of human cargo. With some prodding, coercion, and

Joseph Morgan

other inducements, some tribesmen hunted and trapped others and sold them to foreign merchants.

Cohesive unity among the peoples of Africa was non-existent. The more popular form of government was monarchical. The area ruled, whether family, clan, or village state, was generally under the ruler-ship of a king. The territories and states were not bound together by any kind of federation or mutual consent. Each area was its own sovereign. The tribes enlarged their territorial boundaries by armed invasion of the territories of other tribes, taking captives and selling them into slavery. Thus, the large majority of blacks from Africa who were brought to the New World as slaves, had been captured by other blacks and sold into slavery.

Not all the Negroes who came to this land were slaves. Some were explorers who accompanied Columbus or some other adventurers, others were sailors, and still others were servants. The latter half of the fifteenth century is thought to have been the years of preparation in the history of the slave trade. Spaniards and Portuguese built forts and trading stations along the African coastlines making extensive contact with the natives, and establishing orderly trade relations with them. It was during this period that the Europeans became accustomed to having Negroes do their work for them. Also, during this period, the Europeans developed a rationale for their involvement in human cargo. The Portuguese and Spaniards led the way by invoking the missionary zeal of Christianity to justify their activities along the coasts of Africa. They were chaining people together in concentration camps, removing them forcibly from their homeland, and committing them to a life of hard slavery, and they deemed it a holy cause. In their pursuits they had gained the blessings of their king and their church.[8]

European interest in the New World was in exploitation of the natural resources of the land. For that reason it was necessary to secure laborers as cheap as possible. Indian slavery proved to be unprofitable, mainly because of his economic background, and his susceptibility to the diseases carried by the Europeans. The Industrial Revolution contributed largely to the breakdown of the feudal system in England, and many who were leaving the system signed on board vessels bound for America as indentured servants to

Joseph Morgan

work and earn their freedom in the exploitation of the New World. Others were forced into servitude, but because they were white it was difficult to maintain the system. They enjoyed the right of legal recourse in the land, and many used it extensively. Some others, however, fled their remaining obligations of service to establish themselves in other areas and occupations in industry. The supply of indentured servants was soon exhausted. Then, when an indentured servant ran away it became

> increasingly more difficult, and equally expensive to apprehend them once they had escaped.[9]

The Negro presented far fewer problems. Because of his color, he could be easily apprehended. Instead of indentured service, the Negro could be purchased outright, and there would be no constant turn-over in the master's labor force. There was also the rationale that the Negro was from a pagan land with no exposure to Christian ethics and ideals, and could be handled with more rigid methods of discipline. He would be morally and spiritually degraded to the level of a beast or burden for the sake of stability on the plantation. Black slaves could be acquired very cheaply, and at a time economic considerations were so vital, this was a point of extreme importance. Thus, Negro slavery became a lasting institution, and with the supply almost inexhaustible, there would be no further worries about labor.[10]

So, the raping of Africa was pursued with new and more extensive vigor. The Negro became a commodity, and was hunted down and trapped, traded, transported, and sold into slavery.

From Africa to America

The trip across, called the "Middle Passage," was a long and horrible nightmare. Extreme overcrowding was commonplace. Laws, which were intended to regulate the practice, only amounted to 'showcase,' for such regulations were never really enforced. The slaves were chained together by twos, hand and foot, and there was no room to move about. There was no freedom to exercise their bodies and limbs even the slighted bit. There was no room for standing, sitting, or even lying down in the slaves' quarters. They were simply packed together in chains lying on their sides, and were kept that way throughout the voyage.

Joseph Morgan

There is no doubt that overcrowded conditions on the slave ships was the primary cause of disease, illness, and epidemics. Smallpox was one of the dreaded diseases of that period, and few slavers ever escaped without it. Perhaps more deadly than smallpox was a malady known as "flux." Whites, apparently, were not affected by this disease. It began with severe pains in the head and back, chills, fever, and nausea followed. The disease baffled blacks and whites alike, and was often fatal.[11]

Hunger strikes often aggravated already unfavorable health conditions and induced illnesses where there had been none before. The fifth and stench cause by close quarters, and illnesses that bred illness caused the mortality to be increased accordingly. It is very likely that not more than half the slaves taken from Africa became effective laborers in the New World. Many who had not died of disease or committed suicide were permanently disabled by disease, or maiming in their struggle with the chains. Accurate figures of the actual numbers of slaves imported from Africa are unobtainable. From 1783 through 1793 it is reported that Liverpool traders transported 303,737 slaves. During the following eleven years this figure was certainly undiminished. Franklin (1967) attributes the following estimates to the slaving activities over a four hundred-year period from the sixteenth through the nineteenth centuries: during the sixteenth century 900,000 slaves were imported, in the seventeenth century 2,750,000 were delivered, and in the eighteenth and nineteenth centuries 7,000,000 and 4,000,000 slaves, respectively, were brought here from Africa. These are only estimates and risk the possibility of inaccuracy, but considering the great many who must have been slaughtered resisting capture, and the large numbers who died during the "Middle Passage," plus the millions who were successfully brought to this country, the total number would reach staggering proportions.

It is more difficult to determine the effect of such ruthlessness on African life than to estimate the number of people removed from the land. Slaving activities were carried on primarily in the area of West Africa where civilization had reached its highest point on the continent with the possible exception of Egypt. The ravaging of this great land by savage brutal traders from foreign ports took away

Joseph Morgan

from Africa the flower of its manhood and left the continent impotent, brutally stultified, and dazed. Specifications for the slaving enterprise demanded the best qualities that were obtainable. They sought out the healthiest, the more robust, the youngest, ablest, and the most culturally advanced.[12]

In many of the history books Africa has been labled as the "Dark Continent," the "mother of savagery" where all the rights belong to the man who wields his weapons the best, eliminating any opposition to his exploits. Perhaps the most ironic thing about all this is that history records that the culprit in this whole affair has done all his evil deeds under the banner of the church in civilized nations.

The native sons and daughters of the "Dark Continent," the flower of Africa, who were bred and born into the culture and society, and the religion of their homeland were hunted, trapped, caged, and sold into slavery. They were wrested from that land of their birth and bound in chains for the one-way passage from Africa to America.

Chapter 1

NOTES

1. Peter M. Bergman, <u>The Chronological History of The Negro in America,</u> New York; Harper and Row Publishers, 1969, p. 10.
2. Ibid. p. 1.
3. John Hope Franklin, <u>From Slavery to Freedom, A History of Negro Americans</u>, New York; Vin tage Books—A Division of Random House, 1967, p. 42.
4. Ibid. p. 43
5. Ibid. p. 60 f.
6. Ibid. p. 40, 41.
7. James Weldon Johnson and J. Rosamond Johnson, <u>The Books of American Negro Spirituals,</u> New York; The Viking Press, 1969, Introduction.
8. Franklin. <u>"The Slave Trade."</u> p. 45, 46.
9. Ibid. pp. 47 – 49.
10. Ibid. p. 56
11. Ibid. p. 59.

Chapter 2

THE LOSS OF IDENTITY

When one loses one's identity it is a loss not easy to describe. The idea was to generate animal fear in the slaves, and to instill in them the idea that to be black is to be inferior, to be sub-human. So it was that the slave masters and slave owners sought to dehumanize and depersonalize slaves, and to reduce them to something akin to robots. The loss of identity was brought by a rather involved process. It was something more than the loss of specific individuality, it meant the loss of something intricately woven into the fabric of personhood, it was the loss of the right to exercise the individual will. Murch (1958) discussed the threefold nature of man, and the threefold capacity of the mind. The mind is considered as having at least five attributes: immaterial, unitary, self-active, self-conscious, and abiding. The mind thinks, feels, and wills. That capacity of the mind to think is called the intellect. The ability to feel refers to the emotions, and the mind's power to act is known as the will.[1] Through all the process of enslavement, there was no thought of the human welfare of the slaves. The one controlling thought was that the slave conform to the will of the owner. He was to respond with immediate and unquestioning obedience, and to work at hard labor as the master may order. The combination of all the right qualities, it was thought, would make a 'good slave.'

The Loss of Name and Personality

When a person is convicted of a crime and sentenced to a prison term, that person ceases to be identified by name. He is assigned a number which he must remember and answer to as long as he is in prison. Then, upon release from prison he returns to society with the stigma of an "ex-con." The slave, likewise, would lose his selfhood, as it were. He would be deprived of his most intimate possession, his name,

Joseph Morgan

and personality. In the motion picture "ROOTS," Alex Haley tells the story of slaves who were purchased at an auction sale and brought to a plantation where they would spend the rest of their days. Each was assigned a new name and was required to answer to that name whenever called. Although they could not speak the language, or understand it, they were required to respond in some fashion when the assigned name was called out.[2]

In his autobiography, Booker T. Washington stated that he never knew his father. He did not even know what his father's name was. His mother never mentioned anything of his father to him. It was some time after the Emancipation Proclamation that he learned that he had no sur-name. All he had ever known was that he was called "Booker." When he was allowed to attend a school of any kind, the teacher required all the pupils to have two names; a first, and a last name. Since he did not know of a last name, he chose one for himself; he called himself "Booker Washington." Then, later he discovered that his mother had given him the name "Booker Taliaferro," but that part of his name had somehow been forgotten. Upon learning of it he revived it and made his full name "Booker Taliaferro Washington." With the ensuing years he became known as "Booker T. Washington."[3]

The Loss of Family, Tribe, and Friends

The Middle Passage, (which refers to the trip across from Africa to the New World) and the seasoning process were both demeaning and depersonalizing. Not all fared as well as did Booker T. Washington. Conditions varied from one plantation to another. As a general rule the families were broken up and widely dispersed, so that in the great majority of cases, individuals were separated from each other, and in many instances were completely isolated from all former associations; family, clan, tribe, and friend. The rationale for much of this kind of treatment of the slaves grew out of an underlying fear of a possible slave uprising. It is ironic that it was just this kind of treatment by the slave masters to forestall any kind of revolt, that spurred on and forced the Nat Turner uprising. There was no law that would protect a slave under any circumstance. The slave owner was master, and for the slave, his word was law. For the slaves, there was no recourse; no redress for wrong, for no wrong could ever

Joseph Morgan
be done to a slave.

Frederick Douglass referred to his life as a slave, as "one continuous battle." Professional slave breakers were used by some slave holders to subdue and to subjugate hard-to-handle slaves. As the slave breaker and his cousin set upon Douglass to straighten him out, Douglass resisted, defending himself against both of them, taking no thought of the possible consequences for his actions.[4] There were many like Douglass who through an abiding fear of suffering an unmerciful death, preferred to die fighting rather than a passive submission. Many uprisings were provoked, and slaves would escape from the plantation to join the Indians, and together they would attack and kill the slave masters and their families. The Negro slaves, having no one else to whom they could turn, found a ready ally in the Indians.

Josiah Henson remembered and described the auction at which his own family was broken up for sale to different owners. In his own words he recalls the incident quite vividly:

The Black Baptist Church

...The remembrance of the breaking up of the McPherson estate is photographed in its minutest features in my mind. The crowd collected around the stand, the huddling group of Negroes, the examination of muscle, teeth, the exhibition of agility, the look of the auctioneer, the agony of my mother—I can shut my eyes and see them all.

My brothers and sisters were bid off first, and one by one, while my mother, paralyzed by grief, held me by the hand. Her turn came and she was bought by Isaac Riley of Montgomery County. Then I was offered to the assembled purchasers. My mother, half distracted with the thought of parting forever from all her children pushed through the crowd, while the bidding was going on, to the spot where Riley was standing. She fell at his feet and clung to his knees, entreating him in tones that only a mother could command, to buy her baby as well as herself, and spare her one, at least, of her little ones. Well, it can it be believed that this man, thus appealed to, was capable not only of turning a deaf ear to her supplication, but of disengaging himself from her grasp with such violent blows and kicks, as to reduce her to the necessity of creeping out of his reach, and mingling in the crowd with the groan of bodily suffering, and with the sob of a breaking heart. As she crawled away from the brutal man I heard her sob out 'Oh Lord Jesus, how long shall I suffer this way?" I must have been then between five and six years old. I seem to see and hear my poor mother weeping now. This was one of my earliest observations of men; an experience which I only shared with thousands of my race . . .[5]

During the entire period of slavery, when families were broken up and dispersed, even over wide and unfamiliar territories, slaves made continuing efforts to locate and rejoin their loved ones. This fact is attested to by reward notices posted in southern newspapers. There were slaves who did escape from plantations in search of family members. These—many of them—were tracked down by law officials through known locations of families dispersed over the South.[6]

Slaves were always fearful of being sold into the deep South; Florida, Georgia, Alabama, Mississippi, and especially Louisiana. It was considered by slaves to be a place of slaughter, so those who were bound for Louisiana did not expect to see their families and friends again.[7]   Franklin (1967) the historian has suggested some of the tendencies which served to undermine the Negro family during slavery and the period immediately following. Seldom, if ever, was there courtship preliminary to marriage. There were many cases where the woman was forced to accept the husband who had been forced upon her, and there was very little opportunity to develop any real attachment for her children. [8] Here, Rawick (1972) quotes Franklin's work "From Slavery to Freedom," but disagrees with his conclusion regarding the slave mother's love and care for her children. It was Frazier's belief (1974) that there was abundant evidence, according to Rawick, of the slave mother's devotion for her own offspring. The slave father's role, however, was somewhat less significant, because he was often sold away from his children. The general picture of the slave family which Rawick develops from the Slave Narratives and interviews indicates the bond between the slave father and his children may have been considerably stronger than suggested by other writers. Many of the historical and sociological

Joseph Morgan

discussions on the subject of the slave families have tended to be misleading. The Afro-American family under slavery is seen by Rawick as part of a distinct, viable black culture, adapted to the fortunes, or misfortunes of slavery, separation, and deprivation.

The Loss of Human Rights

It was not enough that the slave as a rule, was generally deprived of the right to any permanent family relationship; to be the head of his household, or family, they were even denied the right to form any kind of independent social contact. The slave had only one right, and that was the right to be a slave; to be the chattel property of someone else, and that someone else, was usually a white plantation owner, or slave owner.

As one looks at the life of the black Afro-American, it must be seen from the beginning that the manner in which the blacks were captured in inter-tribal conflicts and held for the slave ships which supplied the New World slave markets served to strip them, to a large degree, of any social heritage. The slave markets required the young, healthy, and energetic black males and females. The manner in which they were

The Black Baptist Church

held, and transported packed together in the slave ships for the trip across heaped upon them many dehumanizing experiences. They were held at sites that might well be described as the concentration camps of that day, without regard for sex, family, or tribal affiliations. They were 'stored' on board the ships much the same as cargo is stored for maximum space utilization, again without any regard or consideration for age, sex, or human conditions. The black slave became the object of the most brutal, inhuman treatment that could be leveled toward any being, human or animal. Perhaps in modern times, only the holocaust rivals the evils of slavery. There is one important difference: The Third Reich was blood-thirsty, and bent on complete destruction of all Hebrew nationals or kindreds within the state borders, while in America, especially in the South, the white man was seeking wealth and superiority and needed something to stand on. The Jew was not enslaved as was the Negro. Hitler's objective was to exterminate the Jews in Germany, but the Negro was subjected to centuries of relentless exploitation in an attempt to reduce him to the very lowest level of inferiority.

Joseph Morgan

The Negro, in addition to being enslaved, was imprisoned as well. He was denied the social heritage of his culture, he was denied the use of his native tongue, he was denied the privilege of association with his fellow slaves, and in addition to rigorous supervision of his work, he was constantly observed and under the strictest surveillance of all his activities.

The capture, enslavement, the Middle Passage, and the induction into the slave system on the plantation were prominent factors in the destruction of social cohesion among the slaves. Equally important, was the mobility of the slave population. The constant buying and selling of slaves from one plantation to another, and the changing of ownership required the movement of slaves over wide areas in the South.

The Subjugation of the Individual Will

During the slave trading heyday, the black skins were imported into the islands of the Seas, South, Central, and North America at an alarming rate. The great masses of the black presence generated such an uneasiness among the

The Black Baptist Church

whites that the black codes and the slave codes were enacted and became the norm for achieving absolute control over the slaves and all their activities. The one tool that was central, and ever-present, in the seasoning process, and by which cruel and severe treatment was inflicted upon the slaves to reduce them to complete and unhesitating obedience, was the overseer's lash. The lash was always visible, and always in use. The system of slavery unleashed in the white man the vilest, most evil passions. A former slave described some of the equipment used to inflict punishment upon the slaves on the plantation where she was kept. There was a white post in front of the slave quarters with ropes to tie the slaves for whipping. As she recalled, there was a plain strap used for whipping. Then she described a 'wide strap with holes in it,' and a cat-o'nine tails, used for beatings. The slave would be stripped and tied to the post, then beaten with the strap with holes in it until blisters were raised on the skin, then he would be beaten with the cat-o'-nine tails to burst the blisters, after which turpentine and red pepper would be rubbed into the wounds. [9]

Other slaves related stories of varying degrees of the

same kind of harsh treatment of slaves using the rawhide bull whip, the whipping post, or barrel, as the case may be, or stakes in the ground by which some were staked out hand and feet for the beatings. The Slave Narratives, from which Rawick takes many excerpts, contains many stories of complicated and very gruesome punishments used to exercise control over the slaves. A story was told of one overseer whose methods were extremely harsh toward the slaves. He would drive stakes into the ground and tie the slave down stretched between the stakes like a piece of rawhide and beat him till he was raw and bleeding, then he would take brick and grind it into powder and mix it with lard, then he would take the mixture and rub it all over the slave and wrap him in a quilt or a sheet. [10]

The ex-slaves' accounts of their treatment make it abundantly clear that most of the slaves suffered unmerciful beatings, whippings, and floggings; they were often poorly fed, clothed, and housed; that they were often overworked, and that slave women were regularly used as objects of sexual gratification by the whites, slave men were often used as breeding bulls, and slave children were frequently objects of extreme abuse. The whippings and beatings were not only methods of punishment, they were conscious and continuing efforts to impress upon the slaves the fact that they were slaves. They were whipped whether they had done anything or not. They were whipped as a lesson for other slaves; both men and women. If the woman was pregnant, a hole was dug in the ground and her stomach was fitted into the hole, and she was staked out over the hole and then whipped.

The whippings were part of the entire social structure of slavery, and was used as the chief means of breaking down resistance to slavery. It was the systematic means of instilling fear into the slaves to prevent their running away, to enslave the mind and subjugate the will of the slave. Thus, he was bent to the will of the slave masters and plantation owners. The object was to create a docile, contented slave. [11]

The Duration of Slavery

The slave trade had begun at distant ports and worked its way to the American Colonies. Bergman (1969) states that Negro slavery in America was a capitalistic institution.[12]   But slavery also had an economic impact on the New World. Developing the New World and extracting its wealth and produce so that the venture would become profitable was of major importance to a people whose greatest market for industry and produce was the Mother Land. The British Crown extracted the very life blood from the colonies, so that most often when the requirements of the Crown were satisfied there was little left to meet the needs of the settlers themselves. Thus it became increasingly more apparent that in order to fulfill all that was expected of them and still earn a livelihood, they had to produce more and more. This, then, presented a labor problem for which there was no easy solution.

Several options suggested themselves, some of which were tried and failed. Among these were indentured service, where people seeking something better would bond themselves by signing some kind of labor contract to earn passage across the Atlantic to the American Colonies. On arrival, the shipmasters then sold these and their contracts to anyone who would buy them, so that the shipmaster was not left empty. Such people had been slaves to the land in

England; they had been serfs. But with the coming of the Industrial Revolution, they pulled up stakes and left their native land and seeking the promise of golden opportunity and wealth in the colonies.

A second option was to force servitude upon the Indians of the land, however both these plans fell short of all expectations. The white indentured servants had one thing in common with their contract holders; they too, were white. Many grew weary with the tasks they had undertaken, and broke away from the harness of obligation long before their contracts had been satisfied. Then, once having escaped it was both difficult and expensive to reclaim them. Often it was quite impossible to reclaim white servants. Many of them headed for undeveloped territories, or found other employment in industry. The white servant had become a high risk to any who ventured to buy his contract, and was a great liability to the plantation owners. White slavery was deemed unworthy of any further attempts, it was seen as a liability not worth the risks. Great numbers of Indians who were subjected to slavery died under the yoke from disease, exposure, or a combination of symptoms.

Joseph Morgan

The final option open for exploitation was the black skins from Africa. The plan involved great risks which were not limited to economic concerns. Risks with the blacks involved life and property. But since the plan had been made to work elsewhere it was decided to be worth the risk and the effort. It was not difficult to find justification and approval for the new venture. The blacks were from the Dark Continent and were considered heathen and barbaric, thus it was reasoned to be advantageous and beneficial to the black Africans to be exposed to white European culture in the Western world. It was first decided that the black slaves should be baptized, but they were never to be allowed to rise above sub-human standards. Bergman targets August 20, 1619 as the date black slavery began in the American Colonies. On this date a Dutch ship docked at the Jamestown settlement with blacks for sale, both men and women. [13] Their purpose was to help relieve the labor shortage in this new settlement. The number was very small and insignificant by many standards. William Loren Katz (1967) however, takes note of two important events in the history of American Democracy. In addition to the selling of these first African laborers, America's first representative assembly (the House of Burgesses) met for the first time. [14]

Unlike the white man, the black man's skin color made him a prime target for slavery. He was used to agricultural labor, he would be many miles from home and friends, and what is more, even when he managed to escape, the color of his skin made him an easy target for recapture in a land of whites. [15] From this single act the institution of slavery was begun in the American Colonies; the black African was to be used as forced labor in the world's first representative democracy. It constituted the beginning of an era that has left two countries in particular, and many others in general, scarred and devastated for untold generations yet to come.

The question of the duration of slavery is an agonizing dilemma: "how long did slavery last?" or how long will slavery last?" The Negro did not profit from the American Revolution. Its purpose was to break away from domination by the British. The colonies declared themselves to be a union of states, and a sovereign and free nation, independent of British rule henceforward. With the Declaration of

Joseph Morgan

Independence a promising new nation was born. It was a nation born of a desire for human freedom and dignity, whose prominence among world powers will live long in the history of mankind, the land of the free and the home of the brave, became a nation whose founding articles and basic laws of government stood in abject contradiction to its conduct and practice as a free nation. The Constitution of the United States not only condoned slavery, but also legalized, and made slavery the law of the land by act of Congress in General Assembly. It seems quite likely to Bergman that the dominant opinion among those Founding Fathers was that none of the conditions in a system of slavery could ever rhyme with that one basic line in the preamble to the Constitution . . . "all men are created equal . . ." And, further, that the conflict aroused by slavery would one day cause the Union serious problems. For many days, yea even years, prior to July 4, 1776, freedom was the subject burning in the conscience of politician and farmer alike; freedom from the tyranny fostered by the British Crown under George III, absolute domination by England, an Island State, ruling an entire Continent. All of this coming to a head:

The Black Baptist Church

When in the course of human events, it becomes necessary for one people to dissolve the political bands which have connected them with another, and to assume among the powers of the earth, the separate and equal station to which the laws of Nature and of Nature's God entitle them, a decent respect to the opinions of mankind requires that they should declare the causes which impel them to the separation.—We hold these truths to be self-evident, that all men are created equal, that they are endowed by their Creator with certain inalienable Rights, that among these are Life, Liberty, and the pursuit of Happiness.— That to secure these rights, Governments are instituted among Men, deriving their just powers from the consent of the governed,--That whenever any Form of Government becomes destructive of these ends, it is the Right of the People to alter or abolish it, and to institute a new Government, laying its foundation on such principles and organizing its powers in such form, as to them shall seem most likely to effect their Safety and Happiness.

This great historic document, perhaps the most memorable ever published in modern history, gives the basis, the Preamble, and the leading arguments in support of the Declaration of Independence, became the rallying point for the Union Flag, and the Standard for Freedom; the Banner of a freedom-loving people.[16]

Many slaves fought and died in the American Revolutionary War, but when Independence was finally gained and freedom was won, slaves were still slaves. Independence and freedom held out to them neither blessing nor hope. The coming of the Industrial Revolution, and the invention of the cotton gin, the spread of technical progress and the advances in the industry served to establish the institution of slavery, and to make the exploitation of slave labor a more profitable enterprise. [17]

''''So even now, near the close of the 20th Century, this land of ours still bears the imprint of a giant question mark raised by the institution of slavery; how much, how long? The Constitution of the United States was not framed with the Negro in view as being numbered among the recipients of its blessing. The laws of the land even today, effectively exclude the Negro from first class citizenship rights.

The Black Baptist Church

In order to bring the Negro even partially into the framework of the Constitution, required Constitutional Amendments to extend <u>limited</u> rights to blacks. The contributions made by black men and women to the progress of this nation are staggering, and defies comprehension, in

light of what benefits have been reaped from all their efforts. For example, in all the history of this nation, there has never been a black man elected to the Presidency of this nation. There has never been a black Vice President, or Speaker of the House, or Majority or Minority Whip in the Senate. Exclusive social clubs and civic organizations, still bar black membership and black participation. In light of the current events in the political arena, this burning question still seems appropro; is slavery really over?

Chapter 2

NOTES

1 James DeForest Murch, <u>Christian Education and the Local Church,</u> Revised Edition 1958, Cincinnati The Standard Publishing Company, 1943, pp. 111 – 117.

2 John Hope Franklin, op. cit., pp. 55 – 56.

3 <u>Three Negro Classics,</u> New York; Avon Books, 1965, pp. 41 – 49.

4 William Loren Katz, <u>Eyewitness: The Negro in American History,</u> Revised Edition, A Living documentary of the Afro-American contribution to U. S. History, New York; Pitman Publishing Company, 1967, pp. 109, 110.

5 Ibid. pp. 111 – 112.

6 Ibid. pp. 112 – 113.

7 Ibid. pp. 113 – 114.

8 George P. Rawick, <u>From Sundown to Sunup, The Making of the Black Community,</u> Westport, Connecticut; Greenwood Publishing Company, 1972, p. 78.

9 Ibid. p. 64.

10 Ibid. p. 57

11 Ibid. pp. 57, 59.

12 Peter M. Bergman, op. cit., p. 20.

13 Ibid. p. 10.

14 William Loren Katz, op. cit., p. 20.

15 Ibid. p. 21.

16 Henry W. Bragdon and Samuel P. McCutchen,

17 Bergman, op. cit., p. 73.

Chapter 3

THE PERIOD OF TRANSITION

Slavery was not the same everywhere. It is fair to say that some slaves fared better than others. Treatment for some was not as harsh as for others. In states and territories to the North, the slaves' existence was under conditions far less severe than for those in the Deep South. Many slaves feared the possibility of being sold into the Deep South; Louisiana, in particular, which was regarded by many slaves as a place of slaughter.[1]

While some slaves talked of how well they were treated by their masters; allowed to earn their freedom and

The Black Baptist Church

to move about from place to place with less restrictions imposed upon their movements, how their masters had deep consciousness of the wrongs of holding people in slavery and had set them free, gave them freedom papers but they chose to remain with them; others spoke of the increasingly harsh treatment they were receiving for one reason or another; the fear of insurrection or rebellion because of the Haitian slave revolt, the Nat Turner uprising, and the many other incidents that struck fear into the hearts of slaveholders. Slave Codes, and Black Codes were legislated from state to state in order to better control the lives of the slaves, and to safeguard the interests of the masters and their families. Some of the measures taken included requiring slaves to have passes anytime they were off the farm or plantation of their masters, and the pass had to be signed by the master. Curfews were imposed on all slaves; free blacks, in most cases were not permitted to enter areas of some states where slavery was the law, to do so placed them under the same laws as those imposed on the slaves, and they also risked the possibility of being re-enslaved. Then, another measure taken was to have slave patrols to keep a close watch over everything the slaves did. Whether the slaves were asleep or awake they were kept under close scrutiny at all times, and there was no privacy for them. Whenever a slave was caught in violation of some code or law, no matter how slight, severe punishment was always inflicted upon those involved, while others were forced to watch, and were threatened with the same thing if they were caught. This extremely severe and harsh treatment was meant to strike fear into the hearts of the slaves. Fear, however, became a two-way street: while it served to humiliate and humble the slaves into submission to the will of the masters, when driven beyond the limits of endurance, the same fear drove the slaves into rebellion. They would escape into the swamps to become swamp-dwellers, or to the Indian territories to find haven, or band together to kill their masters and destroy their masters' property. Once having taken that extreme, there was no turning back, and the penalty for being taken alive was to suffer a fate worse than death.

As the population in territories increased and they were admitted to statehood, slavery became an issue of vital importance. It was the major source of disagreement in the Constitutional Convention which met at Philadelphia in 1787 for the purpose of drawing up a stronger instrument of

The Black Baptist Church

government for the United States. The controversy centered around two points of the slavery issue; representation and taxation. The Southern states desired that slaves be counted as residents of the states in which they lived but only for the purpose of political representation, and not for the levying of taxes. The Northern states took the opposite position. The compromise to which the opposing sides finally agreed is called the "three-fifths" compro-mise, the slave was to be regarded as three-fifths of a person for purposes of representation and taxation. What this all amounted to was that each slave owned by a master gave that master three-fifths more voice and voting power at the federal level, and for that privilege it cost him three-fifths more taxes per slave.[2] In the enforcing of the Black Codes regulating the lives of slaves and free blacks, the Missouri Code of 1804 made no distinction between slaves and other property. The code also attempted to determine just who was black. It stated that any person having one-forth part or more of Negro blood is to be considered as black and therefore was required to obey the Black Codes. In practice this meant that any person having three white grandparents and one black grandparent is black.[3]

Joseph Morgan

These factors, and many others come together to degrade the black man even more, and conditions of whatever well-being there was in the life of the slave degenerated and deteriorated still more, especially in the South. Under some of the Black Codes, free blacks were re-enslaved by court action. It was feared by some whites that free blacks posed a potential threat to slavery. In light of their fears they waged campaigns of suppression against the blacks in order to "keep them in their place," as it were. Some codes removed any and all distinctions between slaves and free blacks. In 1835 Missouri enacted one of the most restrictive laws against free blacks, requiring county courts to bring before the benches all free Negroes and mulattoes between the ages of seven and twenty-one years and bind them out to be apprentices or servants, bringing them back to 'square one,' slavery by another name.[4] During this period of transition in the antebellum South, tensions were heightened among the slaveholders and the slaves. In the political arena, tempers flared among the representatives of the slave states and the free states. Abolitionists, and non-slaveholders, as well as many free Negroes raised the cry more and more for the abolition of slavery. This would cause an even greater feeling of insecurity for slave-masters, because they stood to inherit a double loss; they would lose chattel property and the investment made therein, and they would also lose a viable source of income.

The state of Missouri gave slaves the right to sue for freedom in 1824. Note that in 1830 the U. S. Supreme Court handed down its ruling in the case of Vincent vs. James Duncan, that the exportation of a slave to a free state gave him his freedom. However, the high court seemed to reverse itself in the ruling on the Dred Scott case in 1857 when it stated that black slaves were not people of the United States, and therefore had no rights which a white man need respect.

The Union of the states began to fall apart over the issue of slavery. The election of Lincoln to the Presidency of the United States tended to bring to a head the slavery issue, as state after state in the South seceded from the Union.Missouri's history of August 1861; notes that the Abolitionist General John C. Fremont, issued a declaration, liberating all of Missouri's slaves. His order, however, was

Joseph Morgan

immediately counter-manded by President Lincoln. Lincoln explained that his only concern was for the preservation of the Union. He is quoted thusly:

> If I could save the Union without freeing any slave, I would do it; and if I could save it by freeing all the slaves, I would do it; and if I could do it by freeing some and leaving others alone, I would also do that. What I do about slavery and the colored race, I do because I believe it helps this Union.[5]

Slaves Searching for the God of Love

In light of the prevalent state of the national and local political affairs, and those conditions under which slaves were forced to live, it leaves little wonder that one of the major concerns of the slaves, was some means of escape. His body could be severely restrained, battered, used, and abused, but his spirit remained a free spirit. His actions were in direct response to the inhuman treatment of his captivity. And, that response made itself known in a number of ways.

Resistance and revolt, rebellion and retaliation, were

The Black Baptist Church

among the more hostile forms of protest among the slaves. The underlying causes of its certain failure were based upon several considerations. Overseers and masters kept the slaves divided and suspicious of each other with the constant threat of mass punishment if anyone knew of any plot of rebellion or escape and did not tell it immediately. Some of the slaves were made into spies and informers with the promise of special favors from the overseers, then planted among the slaves he became the 'eyes and ears' of master and overseer. Other slaves were made into slave drivers, and the more difficult the driver made the lot of his fellows, the lesser and lighter became his burden as a slave. Any failure on his part brought swift and most severe punishment from his masters and overseers. Individual protests took on several forms. A slave might secretly violate what the white man referred to as 'sacred white womanhood.' Those who were caught suffered the most brutal and inhuman punishment, even to the death. Women would sometimes destroy their offspring to lessen the master's profit from his investment in human flesh, while some of the men would mutilate themselves by cutting off fingers and toes, or some other disfigurement that might reduce his market value as a slave.

Some would steal livestock, or kill or maim the master's best livestock. One strikingly cutting incident is the story of one of Missouri's black runaways named William Wells Brown. He had worked on the Mississippi River boats, but ran away and made good his escape; he became an ardent abolitionist, earned a college education, and is reported to have lectured extensively abroad. As the story goes, he wrote a letter to his former master from abroad challenging the law that had committed him to slavery. The letter states in part that:

> The United States has disfranchised me and declared that I am not a citizen, but a chattel; her Constitution dooms me to be your slave. But while I feel grieved that I am maligned and driven from my own country, I rejoice that in this land I am regarded as a man.[6]

But many of the slaves generally found a greater comfort, and means of escape in turning to religion. In his religion he could reach beyond the confines of enslavement in this world to a better life in another world. He found some relief in believing that there was a God of love Who would reward his suffering here with a life of indescribable beauty

The Black Baptist Church

and glory in a land beyond the skies. Thus, he made up songs that would soothe the pains of suffering that he constantly felt; representative of his thoughts were such titles as "This World Is Not My Home," "My God Is A Rock In A Weary Land," "I'm So Glad Trouble Don't Last Always," "Steal Away To Jesus," "Swing Low Sweet Chariot, Coming For To Carry Me Home," etc./

Religion, disorganized, and secret, as it sometimes was, became for some of the slaves, "A Balm In Gilead," a means of surviving through turbulent times.

Streaks of Light In Chains of Darkness

Many thousands of slaves in the antebellum South were denied the privilege of worship at any time, and the penalty for anyone caught was a severe beating. Where the privilege of worship was denied some of the slaves would slip away from the 'big house' out into the fields where they had dug deep holes in the ground and they would get down in the holes in the ground and pray for freedom, for the bettering of their conditions, and for their general well being.

Joseph Morgan

One of the stories that tradition has passed on to this writer regarding an old favorite Negro Spiritual is appropo just here. Katz (1967) observes from the works of Frederick Douglass how the slaves were generally expected to sing while they worked. In Douglass' own experience, a silent slave was not liked by the masters and overseers. In many cases the overseers observed the slaves at work from a respectable distance, so that the group, as a whole, was in easy viewing range. But whether he was watching or not, he required the slaves to make some kind of noise. Tradition has it that on those occasions in the fields while some of the hands were hard at work, others would take turns and go off to the praying ground to pray. If at any time the overseer / master would show up, someone would give the signal by singing "O Way Down Yonder By Myself, I Couldn't Hear Nobody Pray," and anyone who was away from the group could slip back before his absence was discovered.

George P. Rawick has noted numerous incidents from the Federal Writers' Project, 'The Slave Narratives,' of how slaves on plantation after plantation were forbidden to pray, and were not allowed to attend church. In other

The Black Baptist Church

experiences, slaves were permitted to attend the masters' church services. Care was always taken, however, to see to it that the slaves received pertinent instructions on being a good slave; obedient, humble, submissive, and thankful to his master that he is allowed to be his slave. The slaves at the masters' church were merely spectators, and did not take any part in the activities. They sat apart from their masters and mistresses, in the loft, or in a corner in the rear of the church building. When, and if, Holy Communion was observed, the slaves were served last.[7] Katz notes this sermon, written for slaves by Bishop Meade of Virginia:

> . . . Having thus shown you the chief duties you owe to your great Master in heaven, I now come to lay before you the duties you owe to your masters and mistresses here upon the earth. And, for this, you have one general rule, that you ought always to carry in your minds; and that is to do all service for them as if you did it for God Himself.
>
> Poor creatures! You little consider, when you are idle and neglectful of your masters' business, when you steal,

Joseph Morgan

> and waste, and hurt any of their substance, when you are saucy and impudent, when you are telling them lies and deceiving them, or when you are proven to be stubborn and sullen, and will not do the work you are set about without stripes and vexation—you do not consider, I say, that what faults you are guilty of towards your masters and mistresses are faults done against God Himself, Who hath set your masters and mistresses over you in His own stead, and expects that you would do for them just as you would do for Him. And pray do not think that I want to deceive you when I tell you that your masters and mistresses are God's overseers, and that if you are faulty towards them, God Himself will punish you severely for it in the next world . . .[8]

At some points along the way, in the midst of darkness and dismay, disappointment and suffering, some did manage to catch some fleeting rays of hope, that things would one day change for the better. And, for the slave, it could never be too soon.

Slaves and Slaveholders in the Same Church

The Black Baptist Church

Service

For the slaveholders, the ideal arrangement for church services for the slaves, would be to admit them to the same church as that attended by the master. This would be the most logical thing for the masters, because they could always be sure that the slaves would not be taught anything detrimental to the best interests of the slaveholders. At the white churches the masters of religion in Western Christianity, also taught slaves submissiveness and obedience to their masters.

It must be borne in mind that no slave was ever pleased to be a slave. Quite to the contrary, the more the masters and overseers tried to break them and fit them into the pattern of a docile "Little Black Sambo," the more they resisted that kind of mold. Then too, when the slave went to the masters' church he went only as a spectator; he did not participate in the songs or hymns, or prayers, or anything else, except when communion was served, the slaves partook thereof; but always last. Those who chose to attend went just to look on, but for them, the service was empty and

Joseph Morgan

meaningless. Those who chose not to go found something better to do with their time. After a time the masters talked themselves into believing that theirs' were the happy, contented slaves, glad to be their slaves.

Perhaps as one would observe the bondsmen around the plantation for a time, one may get the impression that the slaves have not a worry in the world. They laugh at all the master's jokes when he speaks of the blacks; they laugh when they are being ridiculed, their teeth always showed in a broad silly grin when there was nothing to laugh at, nothing funny around at all. He made a lot of noise most of the time, and in the presence of the master and mistress, he held his dirty cap or hat, in his hand behind his back with his head down and his teeth showing. The house servants; the mammy who nursed the master's babies on her bosom through the day while working at the big house, cleaning, cooking, washing, ironing, and making beds through the day, all the time laughing and talking to herself; the body servants, the handy man; each at his or her own task, laughing all the time, or otherwise just making noise and laughing at themselves. So, many of the masters chatted with their friends or

The Black Baptist Church

associates about the good spirit of their slaves; going to the church and sitting through the service, always happy, always laughing; glad to belong to me.

But it was always the contented slaves, who were more likely to seek opportunity for escape. It is worth noting just here, the case of one, James Christian who enjoyed anything and everything any slave could ever want—except his freedom. He served the family of President Tyler in the White House, was always treated with kindness and generosity, could have as much spending money as he wanted, and lived well. Yet, even this happy slave, seized the opportunity and escaped. Having made his way to the Philadelphia station of the Underground Railroad where he was subsequently interviewed by a Vigilance Committee, his response to the question as to why he ran away was that "he had become enamored of a young and respectable free girl in Richmond, with whom he could not be united in marriage solely because he was a slave . . . So . . . the resolution came home to him very forcibly to make tracks for Canada."[9]

It needs only to be added further, that slaves, especially the plantation field hands—as well as many others—acted the way they did simply because it was required of them to be accommodating. It saved them from the lash many times over. The slave, whose life and well being was never a thing assured, but rested on the whims of the overseer, or master, was never contented with his life as a slave. Going to the master's church did not meet any of the needs of the blacks. It merely served to give the owners more visibility and control of the slaves', lives.[10]

<u>Church Services for Slaves</u>

The masters' attitudes toward slave religion were quite complex in some cases. For a long time in North America there was little concern as to whether the slaves became Christians. As long as they yielded to control without open rebellion and worked well, that was all that was required. Some slaves adopted the outward form of Christianity, but the general neglect as to the content of Christianity allowed them to develop the inward meanings and practices as they themselves saw fit. It has been suggested by many that the emphasis which slaves placed upon religion was to be viewed as a means of finding relief from the daily toils of

The Black Baptist Church

hard labor, and a way of finding some kind of refuge in the promise of a future salvation. Rawick, (1972) can see how that may have been possible had they been generally secular and urban people, and if their only religious expression was dominated by their masters. But, because this would tend to ignore the slaves' own religious experience in the night time prayer meetings and sings, it must be discounted.[11]

From the first, the slaves saw that their attendance at the masters' church services was simply another means of exercising further control over them. Many, therefore would not attend anymore of the masters' services because they never trusted him anyway, and those who had started, just dropped out.

The next thing was to permit the slaves to hear a colored preacher preach to them in the white church. The morning sermon was given by the white preacher. One ex-slave gave this account:

> We went to the church on the place and you ought to heard that preaching, Obey your masa and missy, don't

Joseph Morgan

> steal chickens and eggs and meat, but nary a word about 'bout a soul to save.[12]

Another gave this account of a similar experience.

> On Sunday we all were required to attend the white church in town. They sat in the back of the church as the white preacher preached and directed the following text at them: "don't steal your master's chickens or his eggs and your backs won't be whipped." In the after-noon of the same day when the colored minister was allowed to preach the slaves heard the same text: "Obey your masters and mistresses and your backs won't be whipped."[13]

Again, another means of social control of their lives.

Then, eventually the slaves were allowed to have their own church services, but only under certain specified conditions. The white minister did the preaching, or some white man was there to observe all that was said and done. Thus, most often after church services were held for the slaves, they would slip away off in the corn fields to hold their own services. On such occasions they had their iron kettles and pots into which they would direct the sounds of their voices, so as not to be heard up at the big house.[14]

All these conditions gave rise to what Frazier (1974) has referred to as the "invisible institution" of the Negro church, that took roots and sprang up among enslaved blacks.[15]

Remembering that all forms of social effort was forbidden among the slaves, any independent effort on their part required the utmost secrecy, more often than not, occurring in the dead of night, thus meriting what Frazier termed "invisible".

The Great Dilemma

The white masters told their slaves those things which were intended to make the slaves more responsive to the will of the masters; and make them produce more goods and services in the interests of the estate. They were being programmed for certain responses in manner, activity, and work performances. Church services were empty and meaningless, as they were geared to and directed toward those ends. Now that the slaves were permitted to attend church, the masters sought to divest the church of its Christian content, such as it was, and to invest it with control mechanisms in an effort to maintain tight reins upon them. The order of the day was to keep the slaves in the dark; keep the truth away from them. The controlling interests of the plantation owners was always economic at heart; enlarging his holdings whatever the cost.

Perhaps the greatest fear of the masters was that in those Negro churches organized independently of the plantation church; the white church, was that there were always free blacks there giving leadership, and it was always feared that this would inspire the slaves to insurrection and rebellion against the masters and their properties.

The question which the masters always sought to avoid on every hand was "what would happen if the slaves ever learned the truth?" It was felt that if the truth was ever known by the slaves, they would no longer submit to the chains of slavery. Restlessness among many slaves was beginning to be the order of the day, and an uneasy air of

The Black Baptist Church
discontent began to settle over the plantation.

Chapter 3

NOTES

1 William Loren Katz, op. cit., pp. 113 – 114.
2 Lorenzo J. Greene, Gary R. Kramer, and Anthony F. Holland, <u>Missouri's Black Heritage,</u> Saint Louis, Missouri; Forum Press, 1980, p.10.
3 Ibid. p. 15.
4 Ibid. pp. 48 – 49.
5 Ibid. Foreword, Julius K. Hunter.
6 Ibid. p. 43.
7 George P. Rawick, op. cit., "Religion of the Slaves."
8 William Loren Katz, op. cit., pp. 132 – 133.
9 Ibid. p. 128.
10 Lorenzo J. Greene, <u>et. al.</u>, op. cit. pp. 24 – 27.
11 George P. Rawick, op. cit., p. 33.
12 Ibid. p. 36.
13 Ibid. pp. 36, 37.
14 Ibid. p. 40
15 E. Franklin Frazier, <u>The Negro Church in America,</u> New York; Schocken Books, 1974, p. 23.

Chapter 4

THE END OF AN ERA

Those abiding fears of the pro-slavery states and the plantation owners were well founded. The more slaves came into contact with free blacks, the greater became their desire for the freedom which so many had prayed for, for so long a time. The voices of black heroes and heroines, such as Frederick Douglass, one of the most articulate and outspoken militant voices championing the cause of freedom and human rights for blacks, and Sojourner Truth, a tall, lean figure of a woman, plain in dress and speech, whose unforgettable address entitled "Aint I A Woman," at a Women's Rights Convention in 1851, literally brought the house down

Joseph Morgan

with thunderous applause, tear-stained faces, and cheering screams. Voices such as these commanded attention, and got it.[1]

Harriet Tubman escaped from slavery, and returned to the south nineteen times to lead 300 other slaves to freedom. Thomas Garrett, a Quaker, and one of the conductors on the Underground Railroad, wrote the following letter to one of his friends about her last trip, and had this to say:

> Respected Friend—William Still: I write to let thee know that Harriet Tubman is again in these parts. She arrived last evening from one of her trips of mercy to God's poor, bringing with her two men as far as New Castle. I agreed to pay a man last evening, to pilot them on their way to Chester County; the wife of one of the men with two children, was left some thirty miles behind, and I gave Harriet ten dollars to hire a man with carriage, to take them to Chester County. She said a man had offered for that sum, to bring them on their way. I shall be very uneasy about them till I hear that they are safe. There is now much more risk on the road, till they arrive here, than there has

The Black Baptist Church been for several months past, as we find, that some poor, worthless wretches are constantly on the lookout on two roads, that they cannot well avoid more especially with carriage, yet, as it is, Harriet, who seems to have a special angel to guard her on her journey of mercy, I have hope.[2]

Thy Friend,

Thomas Garrett

The Desire To Be Free

News of all the great events in the Northern Free States, and of the activities of the free blacks, some who had bought their freedom, and hundreds of others who had made good their escape, traveled like wild fire through the slave communities in the South. More and more, they gained the courage to make a bid for freedom. They followed river beds and trails, back roads, and whatever else was at hand that could be used as an escape route to the North. Many of them crossed over into Canada and settled there.

The southerners raised their hue and cry in all the halls of Congress. Violence, and the threat of more violence became the watch-word of the South. It reached all the way

Joseph Morgan

from the deep South into the offices and chambers of Congress itself. Senator Charles Sumner, a New England abolitionist, spoke out in Congress on May 22, 1856, against the strife carried on in Kansas blaming the slaveholders for all the turmoil there, naming some of his Senate colleagues as culprits in the troubles that state was having at the time. The very next day, as the Senator sat at his desk writing, he was beaten into unconsciousness with a cane wielded by Representative Preston Brooks of South Carolina. Reports of the incident carried in Southern newspapers hailed the attack upon Senator Sumner as a grand and glorious deed; as good and very good.[3]

The Southern states raised such a loud and clamorous protest that the North was forced into many compromises in repeated attempts to appease the South and forestall the very ripe possibility of war between the states. Prominent on the list was the Missouri Compromise, the Dred Scott Decision, denying his right to freedom based on an earlier Supreme Court decision which granted freedom to any slave transported into free states or territories. The Fugitive Slave Law was another comprise in an attempt at appeasement.

The Black Baptist Church

The substance of the law grated on the long-suffering of the Northern citizens. The primary purpose of the law was to return runaway slaves to their masters in the South. But it went further than that; it provided slave hunters from the South with legal warrant to enter private homes if it was suspected that runaways were quartered there. The law also provided for strong penalty for anyone caught helping a slave to escape, or harboring a runaway. Six months imprisonment, and a fine of $1,000.00 was quite a stiff penalty. This stirred abolitionists, both black and white, and the cause of freedom for the slaves gained support from many white private citizens whose rights were also threatened by this new law.

Slave Uprisings

The decade of the 1850's prior to the war between the states, saw many upheavals and massive struggles in the tug-of-war to free the slaves. The new law served to intensify an already grave situation. Quakers, black and white abolitionists, Vigilance Committees, made up of former slaves, along with notable private citizens, all joined forces in a common struggle. Katz notes among the many uprisings, some that bore outstanding prominence. One or two examples must

Joseph Morgan

suffice here. He cited the report of a Congressional Committee reporting on the incidence of violence stating that "efforts to recapture fugitives in the North often leads to most unpleasant, if not perilous collisions." President Millard Fillmore also decried this resistance "by lawless and violent mobs." Opposition, however, continued to mount.[4]

Two members of a posse were killed in an attempt to reclaim two runaways who had been caught and jailed in Pennsylvania. In the melee led by a black Vigilance Committee and white abolitionists, the jail was forcibly entered and United States Marshals were attacked in an effort to free the slaves. A mob of Boston citizens bent on freeing slave Anthony Burns in 1854 required twenty-two military units, including marines, cavalry, and artillery to hold the crowd in check.

In 1852, Harriet Beecher Stowe wrote her "Uncle Tom's Cabin," to dramatize the evils of slave life. The book was destined to become a world-wide best seller. Her novel was intended to bring home to all Americans the horrifying and deplorable conditions under which the slaves were forced to exist. Samuel Green, a free Negro, was sentenced to ten years in prison by a Maryland court simply for having a copy of the book in his possession.[5]

Abolitionist Movements

Under the leadership of Senator Steven A. Douglass, Congress passed the Kansas-Nebraska Act in 1854, opening that territory to slavery. Then armed settlers from North and South entered that territory to fight out the slavery issue. Katz reports that one of the slaveholders tried to auction off a slave boy at Iowa Point, and a bloody clash ensued. A group of 'free soldiers' broke up the auction, and a man leading a horse rushed up to the boy and shouted to him that the moment his feet touched Kansas soil he became a free man. Then he ordered the boy up on the horse and the two of them rode off together at a fast gallop, leaving the group to fight it out.[6]

John Brown may not have been referred to in history as an abolitionist, but to be sure, he sacrificed his own life in the cause of freedom for all the slaves. His plan was extreme, to say the least. He had organized a small band

Joseph Morgan

of nineteen men, that included five Negroes, and his own sons. His strategy was to raid the Government arsenal at Harpers Ferry and arm his men; from there the plan included the establishing his headquarters and the Negro Republic of Virginia in the mountainous region of that state. Frederick Douglass recalls having spent hours trying to convince himself that he would be entering a steel trap. Illness alone kept Harriet Tubman from joining the raiders. The assault bogged down, and within hours, it was overwhelmed by marines, led by Robert E. Lee. Brown and his men were tried and convicted, but believing their cause to be just, they each faced death calmly.[7]

All over the North, movements sprouted up to end slavery. Free Negroes, with many whites at their sides, challenged the Fugitive Slave Law on every turn, and at every opportunity.

The First Black Baptist Church

Family ties for the Negro, as well as any social cohesion had been destroyed by the manner in which he was enslaved, and separated from all family ties. Slave traders

The Black Baptist Church held no recognition of any human ties among the slaves. One can recognize that the Negro slave was a lonely man; a "very lonely person," whether man or woman; the slaveholders' innate hatred for the blacks, materialized in the way he treated the slaves; as if they were inhuman, and the lowliest animals were treated better than slaves. Arising from the experience in the New World were such songs as:

> I've got a mother in de heaven, Outshines de sun, I've got a father in de heaven, Outshines de sun, I've got a sister in de heaven, Outshines de sun, When we all get to heaven, we will outshine de sun, Way beyond de moon.[8]

Religion for the Negro, became a solace, for he was a man who walked alone and was in need of some means of escape from the harsh realities of slavery. He found great comfort in communicating with God. Out of his experience of walking and talking with God often came conversion and salvation from sins. But even so, without family ties, the slave became acutely aware of his loneliness in the world, in response to which he could sing:

Joseph Morgan

> Sometimes I feel like a motherless child,
> Sometimes I feel like a motherless child,
> Sometimes I feel like a motherless child,
> A long way from home, A long way from home.

Although formal organization was forbidden among Negro slaves, his religion became the one thing that could not be taken away from him. For without it, he could not have survived slavery. His religion, his adventurous secret hideaway, in his continuing search for the God of love became the means of discovering in religion the needed strength to endure whatever fortunes life, such as it was, might hold for him.

Free Negroes in both the North and the South tended more toward an organized community life. Their interests centered around mutual aid societies and cooperative efforts for economic well-being. These several organizations, including their efforts to acquire general education, were usually the outgrowth of efforts of their churches, where the larger part of their wealth was invested.

The Black Baptist Church

The relations between the free blacks and whites in the churches were determined primarily by the slave status of the large majority of the Negro populace. The Anglican Church had carried on some missionary activity among the slaves, but they had no interest in changing the status of the slaves. The Quakers, however, became the outspoken enemies of the slavery system because they accepted both Negro slaves and free men as equals. They advocated religious training for the slaves in preparation for freedom. A great many Quakers set their own slaves free, and then led the way in removing restrictions against private manumission of slaves. Race relations seems not to have become a real issue in the churches until the great evangelistic campaigns conducted by the Baptists and the Methodists.[9]

Baptist and Methodist missionaries preached and taught liberation of the slaves as part of their creed. Methodists are to be counted among those taking a bold stand against slavery. They required their traveling to set slaves free on grounds that slavery was contrary to divine law, as well as to the laws of humanity. The Methodist Conference in 1784 took positive steps toward the abolition of slavery,

Joseph Morgan

declaring slavery to be opposed to the laws of God, and contrary to the principles of the American Revolution. The Baptists, because of their open attacks on slavery were winning more Negroes in their local meetings. Having planted the seed-thoughts of freedom in the places where they counted the most, both Methodists and Baptists were forced to recede somewhat from their position in the face of strong opposition to their stand on the slavery issue.[10]

Just how the free Negroes and white Christian churches related to each other may be observed in the early activities of the Negro preachers and their relations with the white congregations. The early Negro preachers lived under many restrictions, and were expected to fit into a mold in order to carry on their work. But, whether slave or free, they occupied a dominant position in the religious activities of their people.

The first Black Baptist church was organized in the United States within the 1773 – 1775 time frame, in the heart of the South land at Silver Bluff, South Carolina. Owen D. Pelt (1960) gave this account of the location and founding of

The Black Baptist Church

the church:

> Silver Bluff is located in Aiken County, South Carolina, on the north shore of the Savannah River, twelve miles from Augusta, Georgia. In the 1770's it was little more than a small settlement that had grown up around the estate and plantation of an aristocratic planter named John Galphin.
>
> Our meager records suggest that Galphin was a religious man, and particularly interested in the spiritual education of the Negroes on his estate.

Dr. Pelt goes on to say that:

> History has handed down to us three names associated with the founding of a Negro church on Galphin's estate. We know a good deal about two of them—the Reverend David George and the Reverend George Lisle. They loom large in the subsequent development of the Negro Baptist church. Regarding the third man, we have only his last name. He is known variously as Mr. Palmer and Brother

Joseph Morgan

> Palmer. Ironically, the only certain fact that we have about him is the fact that he is the (founder) organizer of the Silver Bluff Church . . . [11]

These points of history are corroborated by Dr. Edward A. Freeman in his work "The Epoch of Negro Baptists and the Foreign Mission Board." He has documented two sources for his information, "Negro Baptist History," by L. G. Jordan, and Walter H. Brooks, "The Story of the Silver Bluff Baptist Church." Dr. Freeman has appended a personal note, of his visit to the Silver Bluff Church which tend to raise some question of accuracy on the date of organization of the church. He cites the old corner stone of the remodeled building which reads:

> SILVER BLUFF
> BAPTIST CHURCH
> ORGANIZED 1750
> Rev. J. A. Goflin, Pastor
> REMODELED 1920
> Rev. A. W. Vincent, Pastor[12]

Regrettably, Dr. Freeman's findings leave us with some discrepancy regarding the founding of the Silver Bluff

The Black Baptist Church

Church, however, two important facts remain; the Silver Bluff Baptist Church is the oldest Negro church organized by Negroes that history has recorded. And secondly, the church was organized before the civil war. This becomes especially important when we remember the persecutions leveled at the missionaries who dared to risk their lives evangelizing on slave plantations in direct conflict with hostile slave owners. And then too, there were heavy restrictions placed upon the activities of the black church, and it was under the supervision and observation of the whites at all times prior to the Civil War.

Much of the pioneering work of the Negro Baptist preachers had its success in those areas of the South where the ruling class was not so deeply rooted in the plantation system. A goodly number of them preached to white as well as Negro congregations. But there was a question of the propriety of Negroes preaching to whites. There also arose opposition to Negroes and whites worshipping together. As the war between the states approached, problems already in existence compounded themselves. Preparatory to the founding act, Brother Palmer , who was pastor of a church a short

Joseph Morgan

distance from Galphin's plantation, had been conducting evangelistic services for the slaves there, and had appointed one Saturday to hear what the slaves had to say in response to the preaching of the gospel. It is reported that eight came forward and gave testimony. These eight were baptized on the following Lord's Day in the mill stream. Brother Palmer was a white pastor of a nearby white congregation, and the Reverend George Lisle was a former slave, and as the atmosphere of war intensified both Palmer and Lisle were forbidden to return to the little congregation of slaves for fear that their presence might somehow provoke rebellion on the plantation. It was decided that the Reverend David George, a constituent member of the congregation, would take up the mantle of leadership and keep the church together. Freeman's report further indicates that this landmark church thrived there until the "vicissitudes of war drove the church into exile—only to multiply itself elsewhere. Moreover, the work at Silver Bluff began afresh with the cessation of hostilities, and was more prosperous than ever in 1791."[13]

The Emancipation Proclamation

Abraham Lincoln was elected to the Presidency in

The Black Baptist Church

November 1860, and during the four-month interval between his election and his inauguration in March 1861, the seven states in the deep South (Texas, Louisiana, Mississippi, Alabama, Georgia, Florida, and South Carolina) seceded from the Union. Regarding the election of Mr. Lincoln, Frederick Douglass had this to say:

> What then has been gained to the anti-slavery cause by the election of Mr. Lincoln? Not much, in itself considered, but very much when viewed in the light of its relations and bearings. For fifty years the country has taken the law from the lips of a haughty, an exacting, and imperious slave oligarchy. The masters of the slaves have been masters of the Republic. Their authority was almost undisputed, and their power irresistible. They were the President-makers of the Republic, and no aspirant dared hope for success against their frown. Lincoln's election has vitiated their authority, and broken their power. It has taught the North its strength, and shown the South its weakness. More important still, it has demonstrated the possibility of electing, if not an Abolitionist, at least an anti-slavery reputation to the Presidency.[14]

Joseph Morgan

With the Union coming apart, seven states already having seceded, the President sought to make clear his intentions not to meddle in the slavery issue. His primary concern was to save the Union. He published this point throughout the North and the South. To underscore that point, when he issued the call for 75,000 volunteers to suppress the rebellion, Negro students from Wilberforce University went to enlist, but were turned away; recruiting officers told them "this is a white man's war, and the Negro has nothing to do with it."[15]

In an attempt to prevent slavery from becoming an issue in the war, the President and the War Department gave orders that any slaves entering their lines were to be returned, for this was to be a war to save the Union. But the slavery issue would not die. The blacks were persistent however; they kept coming insisting that the Bluecoats were their friends long before emancipation became Union policy.[16]

The President soon realized that he must face the slavery issue, and make some definite decisions regarding

The Black Baptist Church

it. The two issues had thus become joined; the war to save the Union and the war to end slavery became one cause. January 1, 1863, the President, acting under his authority as Commander-in-Chief, issued the famous Emancipation Proclamation. At that time the document did not affect the status of a single slave because it only applied to those areas behind Confederate lines. Even so, the Emancipation Proclamation did change the entire character of the war. From this point on, it became a war to end human bondage.[17]

In areas where the act did not apply Lincoln recommended compensated emancipation, that is in exchange for the freedom of the slaves, their owners would receive a stipulated sum of money. This plan was applied only in the District of Columbia, the nation's capital. Elsewhere, slavery was abolished by the Thirteenth Amendment to the Constitution, which was ratified in 1865.

As the war progressed and Union soldiers drove further into the South, the more difficult it became for masters to manage their slaves. Slave patrols were doubled during the war, but slave unrest intensified. During the turmoil aris-

Joseph Morgan

ing from discontentment among the slaves there were many uprisings. Many were slaughtered for plotting revolts when the plot was discovered, but where one was discovered and put down, many others were inspired by the efforts of those who had died, and did succeed. As the slaveholders were forced into retreat, they tried to take their slaves with them. General Rufus Saxton of the Union Army had this to say of the campaign in the Sea Islands in 1861:

> They tried to take their Negroes with them but they would not go. They shot down their Negroes in many instances because they would not go with them. They tied them behind their wagons, and tried to drag them off; but the Negroes would not go. The majority of the Negroes remained behind and came into our lines.[18]

General Butler of the Union Army started the trend that changed Union policy toward the slaves. Report has it that he was holding three slaves who had fled to the Fortress of Monroe after having been forced to build Confederate defenses. When one of the Confederate officers came to get them, Butler refused to give them up. Since they had been

The Black Baptist Church

used by the enemy against Union forces, he considered them in the same light as guns, ammunition, or contraband of war. He could thus use the "contraband of war" in the Union defenses against the Confederacy. That news traveled fast among the slaves, and within two months, it was reported, that General Butler's post had 900 "contrabands" working for the Union Army. They performed various needed services around the army camps. Many sought to have the Bluecoats teach them the magic of reading and writing.[19]

In light of the Emancipation Proclamation, and the war to end slavery, state after state began to drop, or modify the Black Codes. California and Illinois dropped their codes that denied equal rights to Negroes, and Illinois repealed a law that punished Negroes for merely entering a state. Congress moved to allow Negroes to testify in federal cases, and approved the hiring of Negro mail carriers. With these advances taking place for the Negroes on the Northern home front, new problems arose. The already faultering economy must now absorb a new, and enlarged labor force. Jobs, and funds produced by those jobs were now being directed to Negro applicants where before they were potential jobs for poor whites and other Irish Immigrants. They blamed the Negroes for the war, and resented the competition for jobs. Mob violence broke out, and roving bands of these recent Irish Imigrants, and among them the poorest and most ignorant, attacked and lynched Negro men, women, and children. These rioting mobs were on the rampage for four days, and it took the entire New York City police force, as well as United States troops who had to be called in to help restore order and put an end to the killings.[20]

Slave songs reflected the new mood that began to settle over the entire slave community. "No more driver's lash for me, no more, no more," they sang in secret. In Georgetown, South Carolina, slaves were jailed for singing "We'll soon be free, when the Lord calls us home." Just prior to the end of the war, General Butler said to his Negro troops: "With the bayonet you have unlocked the iron barred gates of prejudice, opening new fields of freedom, liberty, and equality to yourselves and your race forever.[21] The General had spoken too soon. The war was drawing to a close and would soon become history, but the fight for rights was only beginning. When President Lincoln's funeral was

The Black Baptist Church held, Negro troops were left out of the throngs of sorrowing soldiers and civilians who marched behind his coffin. It was only after they had protested bitterly that they were finally allowed march with the other mourners.

The Emancipation Proclamation was celebrated by many people in many different ways. The celebration in the Georgia Sea Islands at the headquarters of Colonel Thomas Mentworth Higginson January 1, 1863 is described in two parts; first by Miss Charlotte Forten, the young Negro school teacher who was working on the Island, and the second is by Colonel Higginson himself:

> The celebration took place in the beautiful grove of live-oaks adjoining the camp. It was the largest grove we had seen. I wish it were possible to describe fitly, the scene which our eyes met as we sat upon the stand, and looked down upon the crowd before us. There were black soldiers in their blue coats and scarlet pantaloons, the officers of this and other regiments in their handsome uniforms, and the crowds of lookers-on,--men, women, and children, of every complexion, grouped in various attitudes under the

Joseph Morgan

moss-hung trees.

The colors were presented to us by the Rev. Mr. French, a chaplain who brought them from the donors in New York. All this was according to the program. Then followed an incident so simple, so touching, so utterly unexpected and startling, that I can scarcely believe it on recalling, though it gave the keynote to the whole day. The very moment the speaker had ceased, and just as I took and waved the flag, which now for the first time meant anything to these poor people, there suddenly arose, close beside the platform, a strong male voice (but rather cracked and elderly), into which two women's voices instantly blended, singing, as if by an impulse that could no more be repressed than the morning note of the sparrows' song,

My Country 'tis of thee, Sweet Land of Liberty, Of thee I sing!'

People looked at each other, and then at us on the platform, to see whence came this interruption, not set down in the bills. Firmly and impressively the quavering voices sang on, verse after verse; others of the colored people

The Black Baptist Church

joined in; some whites on the platform began, but I motioned them to silence. I never saw anything so electrifying; it made all other words cheap; it seemed the choked voice of a race at last unloosed. Nothing could be more wonderfully unconscious; art could not have dreamed of a tribute to the day of jubilee that should be more affecting; history will not believe it; and when I came to speak of it after it had ended, tears were everywhere . . . just think of it!—the first day they had ever had a country, the first flag they had ever seen which promised anything to their people, and here while more spectators stood in silence, waiting for my stupid words, these simple souls burst out in their lay song, as if they were by their own hearths at home! When they stopped, there was nothing to do for it but to speak, and I went on; but the life of the whole day was in those unknown people's song.[22]

Wrapped up in that simple little song by a handful of ex-slaves were the hopes, the dreams, the aspirations, of hundreds of thousands of slaves in generations long since dead and gone. But the dawning of the new day had finally come.

Joseph Morgan
Reconstruction, Constitutional Amendments, and The Bill of Rights

The Civil War had been brought to an end and physical slavery had finally been abolished by the ratification of the Thirteenth Amendment. But while the binding shackles of slavery had been loosed and the black man tasted for the first time the sweetness of liberty, the freedom to come and go at will, to be granted human rights never before realized, yet his problems were just beginning. Freedom was sweet, but it did not come problem-free on a silver platter; these who were finally set free, had known no other life except the life of a slave. Now they were faced with the awesome responsibility thrust upon them by act of Congress which admitted them to citizenship for the first time. They must shoulder the responsibility of earning a livelihood, and making decisions which they were ill-equipped to make, making contractual arrangements, marriage, business, housing, etc., and moving into the mainstream of American life. Many had already begun to use their skills to advance their causes—building schools, houses, churches, etc.,--even before the war came to an end. Those who had not escaped to the North sought to make a go of things where they were,

The Black Baptist Church

in the South, and the deep South. Where he had once been a tool, a beast of burden, he had now become a force to be reckoned with by the Southern white community. The single most difficult fact for the Southern white man was that the Negro was no longer his slave, but his equal. Where he had been the subject of ridicule, fun and frolics, as well as the means of his livelihood, the Negro had now become the object of intense hatred and contempt, and despicable scorn. The plantation owners, businesses and the like, no longer enjoyed the benefits of free labor, now everything required a different approach.

The Negro was now up against impossible odds in the South, yet he did not give up the struggle. One important problem faced by the black community now was the lack of any cohesiveness, lack of co-ordinated effort. This, along with many other insurmountable difficulties, was part of what gave birth to the Freedmen's Bureau. This Bureau organized aid and educational efforts for the former slaves. The plight of the freedmen is difficult to imagine. Andrew Johnson came into the office of the Presidency following the assassination of President Lincoln; as a Southern poor white,

Joseph Morgan

he resented slaveholders, and hated Negroes, and the policies which he espoused encouraged Southerners who sought to impose a different kind of slavery upon the Negro, more degrading, more damaging, more hateful than ever before. In effect, they sought to gag and blindfold the Negroes so that they would become "slaves without chains." What Johnson had said to Southern whites is "how you handle the problems of the South is up to you." Presidential pardons granted to the South was for rebellion against the Union, and pardon meant restoration of land lost during the war, citizenship rights, and aid to recover wealth forfeited by the abolishment of slavery. Thus, what Johnson did was calculated to keep the Negro on his knees.[23]

Two primary objectives of Reconstruction was to deal with politics with reference to the Southern states' governments, political representation and the Confederate debt to the federal government. The other was concerned with what to do with the 'new citizen' who had been a slave, and was now granted a measure of freedom by act of Congress. The term "reconstruction" might logically be applied to the effort to deal with such Southern problems as war damage, lack of credit, and the changeover from slave labor to free. However, during the twelve-year period from 1865 to 1877 reconstruction dealt with two political problems: on what terms the Southern states should be readmitted to the Union, and what should be the political rights of the newly freed Negroes. Lincoln's views on both points were untenable. For the Negro he proposed colonization in Africa and the Caribbean; beyond the Thirteenth Amendment, he was willing to let the Southerners work out the details of transition from slavery to freedom.[24]

Suffice it to say that during all this time the Negro's stronghold was his faith in God, his religion, and his church.

Chapter 4

NOTES

1. William, Loren Katz, <u>Eyewitness: The Negro in American History,</u> pp. 186 – 187.
2. Ibid. p. 185.
3. Ibid. p. 203.
4. Ibid. p. 189.
5. Ibid. p. 190
6. Ibid. p. 191
7. Ibid. p. 192
8. E. Franklin Frazier, op., cit., p. 22
9. Ibid. pp. 28 – 29.
10. Ibid. p. 29.
11. Owen D. Pelt, and Ralph Lee Smith, <u>The Story of the National Baptists,</u> New York; Vantage Press, p. 29.
12. Edward A. Freeman, <u>The Epoch of the Negro Baptists and the Foreign Mission Board,</u> National Baptist Convention, U. S. A., Inc., Kansas City, Kansas; Central Seminary Press, 1953, pp. 27 – 31.
13. Ibid. pp. 28 – 29.
14. William Loren Katz, op. cit., p. 210.

15 Ibid. p. 207.
16 Ibid. p. 209.
17 Henry W. Bragdon, and Samuel P. McCutchen, op. cit., p. 362.
18 William Loren Katz, op. cit., p. 210
19 Ibid. p. 211.
20 Ibid. p. 216.
21 Ibid. p. 217.
22 Ibid. pp. 225 – 226.
23 Ibid. pp. 240 – 245.
24 Henry W. Bragdon, and Samuel P. McCutchen, op. cit., pp. 365 – 366.

PART TWO

THE BLACK BAPTIST CHURCH
I N THEOLOGICAL PERSPECTIVE

Chapter 5

RELIGIOUS LIFE ON THE PLANTATIONS

Should the question be raised as to the most important factor in the Negro's survival of the evils and oppression of slavery, the answer must lie in the black church generally, and the black Baptist church in particular. Such words as "religion," "faith," "hope," "God," "Jesus," and "Spirit" are intertwined and interwoven into one central idea symbolized by the church. His concept of "church," imperfect as it was, gave him the religious experience he needed to bring him into the Presence of God. His faith, hope, and aspirations were capsulized in the theme of the book of Exodus as the title of one of the greatest Negro Spirituals; "Go Down

Joseph Morgan

Moses, way down in Egypt Land, tell O' Pharoah to let my people go."

The central idea of freedom to worship God begins here among people who were enslaved in a strange land. Moses was commissioned to stand before the king of Egypt and command him in the name of the God of Israel; the God of Abraham, Isaac, and Jacob, to let the people go, that they may worship the God of their fathers.

The slave was inclined to see himself in the same light as the Hebrews in Egypt, held in bondage against his will; a stranger in a strange land, a long way from home. Thus, he could relate to this simple, inspiring story in the Bible.

The black Baptist Church may be said to be a child of the Southern Baptist Convention through its missionaries, and has similarities in several important aspects, among which are its doctrinal creed, confession of faith, and church autonomy.

The Black Baptist Church

The first black Baptist Church on American soil was organized among slaves on a plantation in Aiken County, South Carolina. It was founded as a direct result of the labors of white Baptist missionaries. Its theological distinctives are therefore similar to those of the Southern Baptist Convention. At the first, there was little, if any, resemblance to the mother church. The church among the slaves was "church," in name only. There was no local autonomy, no local organization, no freedom to worship. It was church in spirit but not in practice. They could do only what the masters allowed them to do. Masters who were Christian, or who were influenced by Christians, recognized the need for worship and devotion to God, and granted the privilege to their slaves. Some desired the spiritual education of their slaves and allowed them the opportunity to attend church, or revival camp meetings for that purpose. Many others had strict rules regarding the religious practices of the slaves, and these were strictly enforced. The slave was always under observation and did not enjoy the freedom of choice in any matters. Therefore, any meaningful experience on the plantations would have to be secretive. In an effort to avoid detection during their secret meetings they resorted to the use of iron pots and kettles to

Joseph Morgan

muffle the sound of their voices. They held their meetings during the late hours of the night, or early morning hours before daybreak. And, afterwards, they returned to their quarters to be ready for the day. Some were reported to have become overjoyed in the Spirit of the Lord, and they would "holler loud," and for fear of being overheard they would have to stop up their mouths to avoid being discovered at their meetings. In their meetings they discussed the events of the past day and shared their individual experiences, and would comfort each other as they sought to gain more strength to face what the next day would bring.

From such meetings as these the modern black church has arisen and developed. Religious life simple, yet profound. Prayer had a twofold purpose; strength for the harsh realities of the moment, and for freedom to come. That simple kind of religion among slaves was from the heart; sincere. It was far more effective than much of what the practice is for today; superficial, insincere, and pretentious.

Preaching On The Plantations

The colored preachers on the plantations were usu-

The Black Baptist Church

ally those who lived there. They had little education, and had been taught <u>something</u> about the Bible. With the little learning he had, the Negro preacher gave his message with great fervor and zeal, and with the best language he could command. His call to preach came through some special religious experience which would indicate that he had been chosen by God for the special task of spiritual leadership among his people. Through his own personal qualities and distinction he came to occupy a position of great prominence among his people. The weight of authority carried by the slave preacher became even greater when he was licensed and ordained by the white Baptist, or Methodist church.

The one basic qualification which the slave preacher had need of was some knowledge of the Bible. It mattered little that his knowledge was so limited, it was important that he be acquainted with the source of sacred knowledge. On the plantations this had long been the exclusive possession of the his white masters, and his coming into acquaintance with sacred Scripture gave him a degree of prestige in matters concerning the supernatural and the religious, among his fellow slaves. The religious instructions among slaves was

Joseph Morgan

preaching rather than teaching in Christian faith. Preaching was the dramatizing of Bible stories, and of God's way to man. A further qualification which the slave preacher would need to possess was the ability to sing. On the plantation, he was sometimes given a degree of freedom to exercise his talents as a leader among his fellow slaves within certain bounds, and always under supervision.

One of history's finest examples of what the preacher was meant to be, was portrayed in the life and work of John Jasper; born a slave July 4, 1812, and died a free man March 28, 1901. He was called into the ministry at the time of his conversion. He and his master, Sam Hardgrove, were baptized in the First Baptist Church of Richmond, Virginia. His master later became a deacon of the church. Sam Hardgrove was reputed to be a good man, well thought of by his slaves, and had earned their respect prior to his death shortly after the beginning of the Civil War. He gave John Jasper permission to pursue his ministry where ever it took him. He gave him time off to go where ever he was invited to preach, "ole Marse Sam tol' me to fly like an angel, and where ever you go just keep tellin' the Gorspil Story." On the same day

The Black Baptist Church

that Jasper was baptized he preached a funeral the same afternoon. Thereafter, his talents as a preacher were in great demand.

Jasper clung to the secret hope of one day becoming the pastor of a church. He recognized the fact that as a slave he would not be able to give his full time to a pastorate, but he would be happy serving as a pulpit supply for the time being, when and where opportunity presented itself. In due course, he organized the Sixth Mount Zion Baptist Church on September 2, 1867 and served as its pastor for some thirty three years, and was retired from its pulpit by his death on March 28, 1901.[1]

Religious Teaching On The Plantations

Prior to the end of slavery much of the religious teaching on the plantations was calculated to exercise more control over the slaves. Social organization among slaves was not permitted, and their meetings were supervised, or observed by whites. Many zealous missionaries challenged those methods of using the church as a means of controlling the slaves on the plantations, and taught Biblical truths

Joseph Morgan

concerning the love of God, the Fatherhood of God, and the brotherhood of men.

Nat Turner had received the call into the ministry, and had received some training in learning how to read the Bible. His knowledge of the Bible and its teachings merely whetted his appetite for, and increased his desire for freedom. After gaining a small following, he led a revolt against slavery, and began by putting to death his master and his master's family, and putting the torch to plantation property. Before the rebellion was finally put down, a number of other slave-owners had likewise been put to death. Many whites began to recall the revolt of the Haitian slaves that had lasted over a decade, in which Napoleon lost at least forty thousand of his best troops. The Haitian slaves had been inspired by the Declaration of Independence, and the Declaration of Human Rights, or rather of the Rights of Man. In 1791, under the leadership of Toussaint L'Ouverture, and two other black generals, the slaves revolted against their masters. Ironically, it was this successful revolt of the Haitians that shattered Napoleon's dream of establishing in America a great empire dominated by France, and made possible the

The Black Baptist Church
westward expansion of the United States to the Pacific.[2]

The Nat Turner revolt horrified whites all over the South, and for a time the Virginia Legislature discussed the feasibility of giving up slavery in that state. It was finally decided, however, that stiffer penalties and stricter Codes should be imposed. The codes forbade any religious practices by slaves, and denied any and all education for slaves. These codes were rigorously enforced under the threat of death or most severe punishment. Because of codes such as these over most of the South many slaves were, although released from physical slavery, still held in bondage through extreme ignorance because they were denied an education by the masters.

These conditions saw radical changes following the Civil War. Many efforts were promoted to teach thousands of former slaves to read and write, and thus to shoulder the responsibility of citizenship, supporting a family and earning a living. The church, which had been an invisible institution, would now become a visible organism. As churches were established, blacks who were free before the Civil War, and

Joseph Morgan

had acquired some education occupied themselves in every effort to teach the newly freed slaves. Churches doubled as schools, and classes were carried on far into the night. These former slaves were eager learners, and were thirsty for knowledge.

Colored Churches On The Plantations

Plantation churches arose out of a deep need for a means of survival during the time when slaves were forbidden to congregate and hold religious services. There was an abiding fear among the masters that such gatherings could lead to insurrections. Where services were forbidden, they would gather at some appointed place and hold their services by stealth. To guard against discovery and of being overheard they always had their iron pots and kettles. There is some lack of agreement as to the purpose of the pot, but it cannot escape notice that the pot was included in most of the slaves' gatherings during the times when such meetings were forbidden. Some hold that it was a practice surviving their African background, and was believed to provide some kind of protection.[3]

The Black Baptist Church

Many such meetings did occur on the plantations in secret prior to the Emancipation Proclamation. And, since they were religious assemblies, it can be logically concluded that they were religious bodies, or churches. Following the Emancipation Proclamation and the ratification of the Thirteenth Amendment, the secret group meetings became visible and active, some perhaps attaching themselves to the churches of their former masters, and others joining black churches already in existence, or forming new fellowships out of their own religious communities. The coming of the long desired freedom found the Negro unprepared for the vast responsibilities thrust upon him by the abolition of slavery. There were now decisions to be made; where to live and where to work, learning to read and write and making a new start as free people. All these things were very important to the black community. Many of the colored churches also devoted themselves to the task of helping the Negro to cope with his changing circumstances. Many long hours were spent learning how to survive. For many, the churches were the center of community life and activities. Church socials, plays, and dramas, provided cultural development and entertainment. It should be said also, that the black church antedates the Negro home. Long before there was any semblance of a home, there was the black church. All the black man had was his religion and his church, both secret—at least for a time—and both of which he held to dearly. The experiences of the black church were many and varied. The church sought to face and deal with whatever problem arose. Rawick (1977) suggests that the black church came out of three experiences: the slaves' own religion in both its pre-Christian and its Christian form, the Christian churches of the freedmen in the cities, and the white church. Unique in its expression of the black culture, deeply interwoven within the black religious expression, the black church was able for a time to provide some kind of identity for the former slaves in North America.

It was from West Africa that the large majority of black slaves came. And, it was that culture, long surpressed by restrictions of slavery, that surfaced in the religious expressions in the groves and hollows, and in the cabin secret meetings. The black 'mystique' is evidenced in the iron wash-pot meetings of the slaves, as well as in the expressions which vocalized the conversion experiences of many slaves. They were 'kilt ded' or 'struck down by de lawd,' and then after a time there came to them 'a little man,' who brought them through the crisis of judgement. Some were 'ded and in hell when de little man appeared and took them by the hand and brought them out.' Their West African impulse and identity provided the impetus for the struggle against slavery and racism. For a time, that struggle in the South was organized and co-ordinated from the black Baptist church on the plantation. It was that struggle which became the bone of contention between the plantation owners and the black churches.

Emerging Problems of Colored Churches on The Plantations

Slavery in the South did not die easily. It degraded the blacks to sub-human existence, but it was also ruinous to whites as well. It had crippled the white man to the extent that he lacked interest in any kind of improvement, those who may have had tendencies toward industriousness found no place for their talents, and the spinner and weaver, the smith and the shoemaker, the carpenter, caretaker, and landscaper found no place for employment or support. What they could have done was work done by slaves, and as such it was degrading for a white person to do work which was done by slaves. The master's capital is what he had invested in human flesh, and the father, instead of being the richer for the sons he has begotten, is at a quandary to provide for their well-being. The system deprived honest occupations of any diversity, and gave no incentive to enterprise. Labor of any kind became disreputable because it was performed by slaves. For the plantation owners, slavery was everything, and to take it away was to leave them with less than nothing. When the shock of losing the war had worn off and reconstruction came to an end, the South turned to another method of enslaving the blacks. Ignorance and lack of voice on the part of blacks, and the law on the side and under the control of whites became the binding fetters of the new system of slavery.

The black churches on the plantations, by what they sought to do for the blacks, stood in opposition to all the evils of racism, because it was only a new form of slavery, depriving the Negro of the blessings of freedom and equality to which he was now entitled. Churches leading in any

The Black Baptist Church

kind of rights struggle became prime targets for harassment from the whites. Harassment provoked resistance, and resistance brought on what Ginzburg (1969) terms "100 Years of Lynchings." For many years the black family in the South lived in fear of late-night lynch mobs. A Negro could be lynched for any reason; sometimes for a slight remark attributed to him, for looking at a white woman the 'wrong way,' or any other trivial matter. There was no haven, no place of safety or refuge for the black man in the South.

The black church on the plantation was endeared to the Negroes from its inception through all the civil rights struggles, and thus its goals and objectives became the major concern of the whites, and the major source of troubles and ever-increasing problems. While the church as an institution in the South survived through all the suffering 'at the hands of a person or persons unknown,' many of the members were forced to pull up stakes and leave the plantation and the South in search of something better out of life. Some made their way to distant cities in the North, and others sought a means of existence in larger urban areas in the South. No matter where he went, he carried with him his color and his

Joseph Morgan
religion.

Colored Baptist Churches In Urban Areas

The blacks from the South, especially on the large plantations, had learned from slavery and racism the black 'art' of accomodation as a means of survival, and escaping from a bad situation with as little bodily harm as possible. His ways therefore were different from those who had escaped from slavery and gained some kind of education, and as a result were more militant in their outlook. He was different also, from those who were freedmen prior to the Civil War. Finding himself, in some cases, as an unwelcome guest, he would turn to those whom he could find who came from similar experiences and backgrounds, for friendship, fellowship, and worship. The church in urban areas therefore grew out of differing backgrounds and persuasions. The large majority of blacks were aligned with the Baptist Denominations and churches because of the Baptist doctrine of church autonomy in the local congregations. Another point in the Baptists' favor is the practice of baptism by immersion, upon a personal profession of faith in Christ Jesus.

It is true that education, even in its simplest form—

learning to read and write and acquiring a basic understanding of the English language—were a major concern to the black Baptist churches, but there was also concern for moral responsibility among the freedmen, that they now began to take upon themselves the moral rectitude of free, responsible men. They must now adjust themselves to a new way of life, exercising sexual restraints. Now is the time to think and act like a man, become the head of a household, establish family relationships, and become the patriarch of his own family. The years of prior bondage had left an ugly mark on the black man, and the task of rectifying the sins of the past was to be a monumental task indeed.

Patience among the white missionaries ran short and they attempted on some occasions to force the issue. If a couple were cohabiting they were urged to legalize and formalize their relationships. There was resistance to this concept at first. Marriage and institutional family life was not something to be imposed by the white missionaries. A man needed something to call his own; property, or land, or work, or some kind of stability conducive to the establishment of some kind of stable family relationship. This does not describe the pattern of life for all the former slaves. Varying circumstances would alter cases. On some plantations genuine attachments were formed and family structures grew out of them. The 'marriage ceremony' permitted by the masters where regular visiting by a male, or some kind of permanent relationship was permitted, consisted of jumping backwards over a broom together, and sometimes the couple simply stepped over the broom together, backward or forward. In other cases the master questioned the couple as to their intent, and if their answers were satisfactory to him he would simply tell them that they were married and could visit or live together as the case may be, with the understanding that all assigned duties must be performed, and children born out of the marriage would become the property of the mother's master. Thus, a continual labor of love in teaching Biblical principles became the task of the black church right in the community where they lived and worked. When freedom came some tried to locate their families and make new beginnings as families by choice. Where this was not possible, the black church sought to help men and women set new directions and offer new perspectives on life as a free human being. Many black preachers and pastors who had been

The Black Baptist Church

slaves now gave themselves wholly to the study of the Bible. They worked long hours, studying and ministering as best they could under their circumstances.

Dubois (1903) portrayed the black preacher as evolving from the West African background of Priest or Medicineman in his early appearance on the plantation and functioning as healer of the sick, and interpreter of the Unknown, the comforter of the sorrowing, supernatural avenger of wrong, and one who expressed in picturesque terms the longing, disappointment, and resentment of a stolen and oppressed people. This personage, described as bard, physician, judge, and priest within the narrow limits permitted by the system of slavery, surfaces as the Negro preacher. And, under him, and guided by his influence arose the first Afro-American institution, the Negro church. Dubois further notes that the church was at first void of both organization and Christianity. Assemblies were voluntary, they were drawn together by their common lot, sharing their experiences, and singing and praying together. There may have been, as Dubois intimates, the mingling of various ancient rites from somewhere in their past, but in the course of time there was exposure to

Joseph Morgan

the churches of the masters, the efforts of white missionaries, and at the most crucial point in the founding of the black churches, the black preachers on a daily basis, living among the people, sharing their life-experiences, understanding their feelings, their hurts, their needs; all of this was well in its place, but the actual birth and growth of the black church in its totality must be attributed to the work of the Holy Spirit using men to the glory of God to accomplish God's purposes.

The black Baptist church, rising from the dust of degradation and deprivation stands forth now under the banner of freedom to assume its rightful place of leadership, to give direction and meaning to the lives of black and white alike, to touch the lives of unborn generations, as a light in a dark world. It may well be said that the Afro-American home was born out of the black church. The missionary zeal of the church was born out of the needs of its own people among whom it was formed. It set before them the Biblical Standard by which men must live if they would please God. It sought to lift their sights, and help them adjust to life and circumstances as they met them.

Chapter 5

NOTES

1. Richard Ellsworth Day, <u>Rhapsody In Black, The Life Story of John Jasper,</u> p. 138.
2. Lorenzo J. Greene, et. al., op. cit., pp. 12 – 14.
3. George P. Rawick, op. cit., pp. 41 – 42.

Chapter 6

ASSOCIATIONS OF "COLORED" BAPTIST CHURCHES

The interests of black Baptist churches were not limited to religion alone. They were also interested in the morality and economic well being of the people they served as well. Mutual aid societies were also formed by the churches. These were concerned with providing aid to families in dire straits, in times when sickness overtook the chief breadwinner in the family. The purpose of an organization or concern was generally indicated by its name. Such groups were formed to meet the crises of life such as sickness and death, and were known as "sickness and burial" societies. Many of the leaders in these ventures were the preachers around which the congregations assembled themselves. As preachers, the large majority of these men were endued with the ability to govern men, and to marshall support for suffering humanity. Men such as these, who were pastors of the churches, also served as community leaders.

After the Emancipation the black churches in the

South, and even prior to that time in the North, began to sever their ties with the white churches, either by their own choosing, or by compulsion. The Methodist churches, by virtue of their doctrinal foundations, were compelled to unite for purposes of Episcopal government. Baptist churches, however, became independent, self-governing bodies. They pooled their meager resources to buy buildings and the lots on which they stood; others would buy the land and erect buildings suited to their needs. Some of the members of the churches had become skilled craftsmen and artisans, including the minister, in a number of cases, and they were able to do much of the needed work and services themselves. The churches in the communities motivated by the desire to achieve common goals were effective in much that was done for the good of the local community. It was

Joseph Morgan

discovered that much more could be done working together than when people worked alone. The people learned to pool their resources, their monies, talents, skills, services, etc., and this gave them the impetus to tackle the impossible and accomplish almost any task. People and the churches comforted each other, and strengthened each other through those early struggles.

An amazing number of black preachers distinguished themselves serving sometimes, mixed congregations, other times black, and still other times, white congregations as pulpit supply, or pastor or as evangelist. In due course they were allowed to purchase their freedom and to pursue seminary training in some of the white Baptist seminaries. It would be inspiring indeed, to enumerate some of the accomplishments of outstanding black ministers and the congregations that gather around them, especially when one considers that these beginnings were undertaken among slaves, unto whom the right of assembly was expressly forbidden.

Socially, the black man's area of activities and functions were circumscribed by the color of his skin. His social

The Black Baptist Church

contacts were members of his own race, and quite often limited to his church activities. The need arose out of these factors for extending the range of effectiveness of the church, and to broaden its contact with sister churches. The Association of churches was not totally new to the black churches, for many of the members of the black Baptist churches had held prior membership in the white Baptist churches and to some extent were acquainted with the kind of strength and influence that can accrue from such a fellowship. For the black churches the idea of association was to provide an expanded fellowship of sharing in at least four areas.

Sharing Common Experiences

In the associations of churches, the membership-churches were usually grouped in certain geographic areas; a given city, or county, or an outlying area within the state.

The years before the Civil War saw strides of progress in areas of the new American West, which included the state of Ohio, as well as Illinois, which at the time were known as frontier states, and it was to these areas that many slaves and freedmen fled and found there conditions highly

Joseph Morgan

favorable for worship in the churches of the Baptist faith. Black Baptist churches had been established in Pittsburgh, Buffalo, Cleveland, Columbus, Cincinnati, Detroit, and Chicago, and soon there were more black Baptist churches in the New West than anywhere else in America. Black Baptist churches had been in existence far longer in the North and in the South than in the new West, even so, it was in the West that the first associations of black Baptist churches were formed. Pelt (1960) attributes this fact to the vast expansion of the frontier, distance, and loneliness that brought about a need for communication between the churches.

Pelt, again notes, that the first association of black Baptist churches was formed by the black Baptist churches in Ohio; Providence Baptist Association in 1836, and was the oldest forerunner of the National Baptist Convention. Two years later black Baptists of Illinois founded the Wood River Baptist Association. Later, in 1853, these two organizations along with black Baptist churches in other Western states decided to establish a single body to promote their mutual interests, and organized the Western Colored Baptist Convention.[1] The great significance of this movement was

The Black Baptist Church

that it brought together a large enough group of churches to become a real factor on the national religious scene.

The common interests and aspirations of these churches as individual groups of Christians may have traversed many divergent paths, but one fact common to all of them is that they were all colored. Their common experiences included at least two points with regard to their membership: one is that they were all former slaves or children of former slaves, and had been set free, or had bought their freedom somehow. This fact alone would account for a significant portion of the membership of the churches. Another fact common to all the member-churches is that many of the members were runaway slaves who had escaped captivity in the South and found refuge in the North and West. The one asperation, common to all of them was the burning desire to see the end of slavery.

The haven in the North and West for runaways was only temporary, for in 1850, Congress enacted the fugitive slave law as a last resort in an attempt to prevent a shooting war between the North and the South. Some of the provisions of the Act required anyone knowing the whereabouts of runaways to report that fact to the authorities so that the slave could be returned to his lawful owner. It also gave slave hunters legal warrant to enter the homes of anyone suspected of harboring runaways, and conviction could bring fines as well as prison terms with the risk of possible confiscation of some, if not all, their property. Thousands of white Northern citizens, angered and intimidated by the new law, armed themselves against any slave hunter who might dare to trespass on their properties. Many others simply ignored the law. Runaways, however, were very much unsettled by the law because they never knew when someone might turn them in. Many therefore, pulled up stakes and crossed the border into Canada.

The Fugitive Slave Law came as the only interruption to the rapid growth of the Western Baptist churches. The most immediate result of this new exodus was the establishment of the Afro-American-Canadian settlements across the Southern portion of the Dominion of Canada. With these new black settlements came the black Baptist churches.

Sharing Learning Experiences

The missionary work of Lott Carey in Liberia, had not been forgotten by the black Baptist churches. One of the major goals of the churches was large scale missionary work in Africa, sponsored by the black Baptist churches in the United States. With this goal in view, a group of black Baptist churches New England and Middle Atlantic states organized the American Baptist Missionary Convention. During the life of the convention, several missionaries were sent to Africa for brief periods. But for the lack of experience and funds, they were unable to pursue long range endeavors in the field of missions in Africa. After twenty-six years the convention finally merged with another foreign missions convention and became the predecessor of the Foreign Missions Board of the National Baptist Convention. Prior to the merger, the most important accomplishments of the convention was on American soil. The twenty-third Annual Session of the convention was held in Washington, D. C. in 1863, and a committee on Resolutions was authorized to seek an audience with President Lincoln to present the convention's plans for voluntary missions in the South

Joseph Morgan

among newly freed slaves. Their desire was to travel south with the Union armies and serve as teachers and ministers to help the freed slaves to get off to a new start as free men and women. The President's response was positive, and the ministers were graciously received and welcomed by the freed blacks, Their work was attended with substantial success in the South. This phase of the work of the convention was a shared venture of all the churches. The task of lifting the blacks from the depths of total ignorance was a mammoth task indeed, and drew together a host of determined and dedicated workers from all quarters.

In Pelt's reflections he notes the significant contributions of four groups that were necessary to make this operation a successful and worthy venture. Measurable progress was to be observed at each of four stages. In these stages there were dedicated white people from the North and from the South, teaching, instructing, tutoring, building schools, etc., helping where help was needed, applying themselves in selfless devotion to a task that required all the virtue that could be mustered by courageous people. Then, the Negro himself, was involved in the very heart of the plan. The

The Black Baptist Church

graduates from the early schools and colleges invested the learning and capabilities they had acquired in those early days of the operation, as teachers, administrators, and even as presidents and trustees of the colleges. Then they began to found new schools on their own. Then too, they also made significant financial contributions to the maintenance and enlargement of the existing schools. A fourth consideration brings the churches into focus regarding this mass educational effort. A general overview of past history shows the churches in the very heart of this educational struggle, bearing the greatest burden of this effort, were churches and church groups, and associations of churches. Among these churches and groups, Baptist churches played the greater role. And in the third stage of the operation, no Negro church played a greater part than the Negro Baptist church.

Dr. Pelt has referred to this era following the Emancipation of the Negro as Operation Bootstrap, and paid particular note that it was the Baptist church in general, and the Negro Baptist church in particular, at the core of this movement, and the size, scope, and good, accomplished, for the glory of God, and the benefit of humanity will never be measured by men as long as time shall last.² The story of the churches' involvement in the effort to educate almost the entire black populace that they might become a viable community of free citizens is of such magnitude that the greater portion of the story must remain untold. The churches' purpose was twofold: teaching the three 'R's; life skills, and furthering the Word of God in the black community. Through all these crucial times the black Baptist churches presented themselves forthrightly as a caring fellowship, sharing their limited resources and learning experiences.

Sharing in Community Revivals

The decades of the 1720's and the 1730's saw the beginning of the Great Awakening in the English colonies of America. Inspired by John Wesley's stirring experiences in the evangelistic campaigns that he led in London, England; marking the beginning of Evangelical Revival, it was also the precursor of the mass movements which revitalized the Protestant churches, bringing into them an increasing proportion of the partially de-Christianized population.³ Robert G. Torbet (1950) notes that the spirit of evangelism permeated the thirteen colonies about mid-18th century, vital and

The Black Baptist Church

alive with emotionalism, and conversions based on conviction of sins was the result in men, women, and children. But this was followed by a period of spiritual decline. It was toward the end of the 18th century that revival fires were again fanned into flame by a call to prayer for revival, which was met with "enthusiastic approval" from evangelical Christendom thus beginning a new evangelistic drive that was to last into the 19th century.

It was during this wave of evangelism that swept through the colonies in the 18th and 19th centuries that the white evangelists and missionaries began their work among slaves on Southern plantations where ever the masters would permit them to go and work. When laws were passed in the South that assured slaveholders that a slave's conversion to Christianity was not a means of gaining freedom, more masters were willing to permit their slaves to hear preaching by the missionaries. In many cases it was permitted only under observation and strict control. Even so, the Negro was caught up in the movement.

George Lisle, a Negro slave, became the first Baptist

Joseph Morgan

preacher to carry the gospel of Christ to a foreign land, antedating the work of William Carey by at least fifteen years. He was granted freedom by his owner, a deacon in one of the white churches in Savannah, Georgia, that he might devote his full time to preaching. His devotion to the study of the Word, and to his preaching ministry secured for him opportunities to speak to white congregations, one, of which he was a member. He worked also with Elder Palmer in founding the Silver Bluff Baptist Church, later, to become its pastor; and also was founder of the first African Baptist Church of Savannah, Georgia, and was its pastor until the evacuation of that city by the British. Following the death of his former master, Deacon Henry Sharp, the Sharp heirs sought to re-enslave Lisle. At this point he borrowed money to remove himself and his family from their reach. He moved to Jamaica where he held preaching services among Negroes there, and during the first eight years of his ministry in Jamaica he baptized five hundred Negroes. He repaid the loan for his move to Jamaica by serving as an indentured servant. Through his efforts a chapel was erected at Kingston in 1789, according to Torbet (1950), so also Jordan (1930).

Lott Carey, David George, John Jasper, Thomas

Paul, Andrew Bryan, Josiah Bishop, and countless others whose untiring devotion in the cause of Christ among black people can never be forgotten. The urgency of their message moved great masses of Negroes to accept Christ as their Savior and Lord.

Sharing In Missionary Emphasis

To emphasize the nature of their work and the purpose for which they were founded, thousands of black Baptist churches and organizations have adopted "missionary" as part of the name of their church or organization. The name, Lott Carey, like that of William Carey, is synonymous with missions. There have been others, of whom history has told us little, but were used of the Lord, nonetheless, as missionary building blocks during critical times and in far-off lands under most severe circumstances. Part of the vast scope of the missionary enterprise was the preparation of leaders who would work among the members of the race to raise the standard of Christ among the people.

Following the Emancipation the assistance contributed to the Negro causes by white churches was mostly edu-

Joseph Morgan

cational assistance. For some years after the Civil War the white churches in the South were virtually impoverished by that conflict, and were lacking in financial resources to offer much assistance to freed men. In contrast, the churches in the North felt a pressing obligation to do something, and had the means to do so. It was by their conviction, according to Latourette (1953), that the most good could be accomplished by concentrating their aid and assistance in furthering the preparation of Negro leaders who in turn would apply themselves to the great task of lifting and advancing the black race in America.

The American Missionary Association, founded in 1846 by white churches in the North, maintained theological schools to provide an educated ministry. When state governments in the South were able to establish schools in the elementary and lower grade levels, the American Missionary Association set itself to build institutions of higher learning from the secondary level and up. Some of the outstanding institutions which they inaugurated were the Hampton Institute, Atlanta University, and Fisk University.

The Negroes were deeply involved in their own

The Black Baptist Church

causes also, and made great strides forward in the field of education, the main thrust of which was advanced through the churches. Booker T. Washington, who received the major portion of his education at Hampton Institute , was the chief instrument in the founding of Tuskegee Institute at Tuskegee, Alabama, which Latourette (1953) refers to as being one of the most progressive in fitting the Negro to improve the life and standards of his community.

Chapter 6

NOTES

1. Owen D. Pelt, and Ralph Lee Smith, Op. cit., pp. 67 – 69.
2. Ibid. pp. 127 - 148.
3. Kenneth Scott Latourette, <u>A History of Christianity,</u> New York; Harper & Row Publishers, 1953, p. 827.

Chapter 7

COLORED BAPTIST CONVENTIONS

The development of some kind of denominational unity among black Baptists found its base in a strong motivation toward missions. The Providence Missionary Baptist Association of Ohio, founded in 1836, the first black independent organization of churches in America was followed three years later by the organization of the Wood River Baptist Association of Illinois. These two Baptist bodies became the forerunners of what was later to become a national parent organization of black Baptist churches and associations as well as statewide organizations.

The controlling interests of such an organization were to be missions and education. As separate groups their purposes were being defeated in duplication of efforts. With the organization of such independent groups of black churches, the black Baptist church was finally coming of age. It was moving into the main stream of the national religious scene, and to make its influence felt where before it had been all but ignored. The church, for the large majority of Negroes, was still the focal point of life and culture for the black community. The church provided a platform for expression, and opportunities for developing talent; developing leadership abilities, communicating thoughts, rhetoric and oratory. The black church restored the Negro to humanity and personhood. It gave him identity and individuality. What home there was for him the church had been instrumental in its establishment. For many years it could be said that home and work were places where he could be found, but church was where he "lived." He learned to apply himself to the task of earning a livelihood, but only in and through the church was he genuinely alive and vital. The church, having done so much in the past, now looks ahead.

Missionary and Education Conventions

The work of Lott Carey in Liberia, West Africa was never forgotten by the black Baptist churches. It fired the zeal of a great many black churches. It became the goal toward which they directed time, talent, and means, and provided needed inspiration for those who would spearhead missionary drives emphasizing the need for support of those who would answer the missionary call.

Black Baptist churches in the New England and Middle Atlantic states combined their forces in 1840 to establish the American Baptist Missionary Convention. Its life span was a total of twenty-six years. The group then elected to merge with other foreign mission conventions whose organization antedated their own. These combined conventions formed the Consolidated American Baptist Convention. This then, became the predecessor of the Foreign Missions Board of the National Baptist Convention. The organization of this convention in 1866 which Dr. Freeman's work (1953) notes as the Consolidated American Baptist "Missionary" Convention-[quotes placed by this writer to show inclusion

Joseph Morgan

of this word as part of the actual name of this organization], served to unite the efforts of most of the black Baptists in all sections of the country. Available records at Sunday School Publishing Board of NBC. USA., Inc., show that the life of this convention extends to 1879, the year before the founding of the Foreign Mission Convention. According to Freeman's research (1953), this convention met triennially, but its Executive Board held its sessions <u>annually</u>, and kept the constituency informed of its proceedings through the official organ, "The National Monitor."

Their annual meeting, which convened in New York in November 1876, was said to be quite impressive. Financial aid was distributed to forty-six schools, and eighteen new schools were organized, and over five hundred baptisms were reported for the year. Delegates were in attendance from fourteen states, and reports were given of the work in Haiti.

The following year, 1877, twenty-six states reported a total enrollment representing 600,000 Negro Baptists. The convention considered proposals to erect a new edifice at

The Black Baptist Church
Port au Prince. The convention also voted to meet annually instead of triennially.

At the meeting of 1878 the Committee on Foreign Missions recommended the formation of a Foreign Board, Dr. Freeman continues, the plan was adopted and officers were chosen to head up the work and co-ordinate all missionary efforts. In addition to the Haiti Missions, the convention extended its missionary arm to Africa, naming the Reverend C. H. Richardson as missionary to the new field. Chicago was chosen as the site for the Board's headquarters, and the Reverend Richard DeBaptiste of Chicago was chosen as corresponding secretary. Receipts for the year totaled over $3,600.00.

In the report of the Committee on Education, the need for an educated ministry was seen as a matter of great urgency. Their plea was that the ministry would pursue specialized training in those areas consistent with their work, and they were commended to schools in the North and South that were open to qualified black applicants.

Joseph Morgan
Regional Conventions

These bodies may be described as a convention composed of independent Baptist churches and organizations from two or more states. These have been alluded to above. Torbet (1950, 1963) notes the organizing of yet another convention in Washington, D. C., in 1893, known as the Baptist National Education Convention. Each of these have their places in a long chain of events making their contributions to advance the cause of Christ among the black Baptist people across the country. With the growth of church membership among the black Baptists, and the increase of the number of member-churches in the associations, the feasibility of continuing multi-state regional conventions was no longer considered a viable option, and with this view the regional conventions lost their appeal. As the existing conventions combined with other bodies to form, as it were, a stairway to one national organization of black Baptists, the regional concept vanished from history, and in its place came the state organizations.

State Conventions

The state conventions styled their organizations

The Black Baptist Church

on a par with the national parent body. The make-up of the state conventions consisted of independent black Baptist churches, Baptist district associations, and other Baptist groups. The convention's work was departmentalized according to the departments or auxiliaries of the churches with some modifications and adaptations according to the requirements of the particular state organization. The Thirteenth Amendment abolishing physical slavery had been ratified in 1865, and one year later in 1866, the Consolidated American Baptist Missionary Convention was formed. Then, only twelve years later—twelve years following the emancipation—this convention reports a total of twenty-six member-state conventions, representing a membership of 600,000 black Baptists combining their forces and organizing their efforts into a unified work on a national scale. The magnitude of such a miracle can only be appreciated when viewed in light of the obvious stern restrictions imposed by law in the slave states in the South, and the Fugitive Slave Act that seriously threatened the churches in the North.

The Missionary Baptist State Convention, of which the writer presently {at the time of this writing} served as

Joseph Morgan vice president, was organized on October 8, 1888 at the Second Baptist Church of Chillicothe, Missouri. The process which culminated in the founding of the Missouri state convention began with a twofold purpose in view: first, there was a desire to improve the general condition of the colored Baptist churches in the state; and, secondly, there was a zeal to establish a school of religion for Bible study. When the call went forth announcing a meeting date for April 12, 1888, to be held at the Morgan Street Baptist Church of Sedalia, Missouri, prominent Baptist ministers of the state assembled in answer to that call to discuss the subject matter. The ultimate result was the birth of the state organization bearing the name of the General Baptist Association of Missouri. It was to be named later, "The Baptist State Convention of Missouri," and is currently identified as "The Missionary Baptist State Convention of Missouri." The officers chosen to lead the convention through its formative years were:

    President---------------------Reverend J. T. Caston
    First Vice-President--------Reverend William J. Brown
    Second Vice-President----Reverend J. T. Thornley
    Recording Secretary--------Reverend J. S. Corsey
    Treasurer---------------------Reverend Daniel S. Sawyer

The Black Baptist Church

The convention affiliated with the National Baptist Convention USA, Inc.

The first president served a total of 34 years. The eighth president, Dr. I. H. Henderson, Jr. (with whom the writer served as vice president) was elected to that post at the Annual Session of the convention in 1962. He was a man highly honored by the constituency of the convention, and the 1981 Session will mark the completion of nineteen years of faithful and devoted service to the black Baptists of Missouri.

The composite structure of the convention consists of the black Baptist churches which make up the member-district associations and auxiliaries of the convention.[1]

National Organizations

The missionary motive became a central core around which black Baptists moved toward denominational unity. The zeal for missions was the underlying purpose which brought into existence the first independent organization of black churches in America, the Providence Missionary Baptist District Association of Ohio in 1836. Then, within

Joseph Morgan

four years of that date, two other independent organizations of black churches had come into existence; the Wood River Baptist Association of Illinois in 1839, and in 1840 the American Baptist Missionary Convention was organized under the torch of a missionary zeal.

The next significant milestone was the merger of Providence and Wood River into the Western Colored Baptist Convention in 1853. During the Civil War the American Baptist Convention began falling apart, and in 1866 the better choice of wisdom was to merge their remaining programs and assets with the Western group, then the name of "Consolidated American Missionary Baptist Convention" was adopted. Pelt (1960) endearingly refers to these old organizational names as fossils in a historian's showcase, but these are more than mere fossils. They are more like rungs of an invisible ladder, like risers in the world-arena upon which the race has climbed from the wretched degradation of an enslaved past to the plateau upon which the black church is now poised, engaged in the present, and looking to the future. They are part of the foundation upon which the black Baptist church stands today. We stand upon the shoulders

The Black Baptist Church

of countless heroes of the past, both black and white who have borne the lash of the whip as part of the price for the privileges we enjoy today. The burdens which were borne by that host of pioneer Saints of the past places upon us today an awesome task; a debt which cannot be repaid except as we give ourselves in selfless devotion to those causes of Christ to which they were espoused, so that unborn generations here and around the world shall know the Truth, shall have a saving knowledge of Christ because of us—because of them.

The Reverend W. W. Colley, a native born Virginian, and black missionary to Africa under the auspicies of the Foreign Mission Board of the Southern Baptist Convention was one of the key figures in the organization of the Baptist Foreign Missionary Convention at Montgomery, Alabama in November 1880. He returned from Africa according to Dr. Pelt (1960), in 1879 with a deep conviction that the black Baptist churches had an impelling role to play, an imperative obligation to become more actively involved in a missionary enterprise embracing the needs of the black people in Africa. He shared that conviction with the Colored Baptist Conven-

Joseph Morgan

tion of Virginia. The convention retained Colley to launch a massive effort to assemble a general convention of black churches to examine more closely the problem of foreign missions.

The Reverend Colley, serving as chairman pro tem, of the meeting, called the group to order on the morning of November 24, 1880. Colley stated the purpose of this meeting to which 151 delegates had been called, and the group went to work. On this historic occasion the Foreign Mission Convention of the United States of America was formed. Dr. Edward A. Freeman, President of the Missionary Baptist State Convention of Kansas, and the executive head of the Congress of Christian Education of the National Baptist Convention USA., Inc., has done extensive research in the area of foreign missions. His work has been cited at many points herein. Freeman, in pursuing his subject, went to Montgomery, Alabama in 1951 and conducted personal interviews with members of the First Baptist Church where the Foreign Mission Convention was organized, and who were eyewitnesses of the proceedings. The weight of their testimonies bears quoting.

The Black Baptist Church

Freeman's approach was to speak with the then present pastor of the church, the Reverend Alfred Louis Bratcher, who stated that

> The Foreign Mission Convention was organized in the First Baptist Church, during the pastorate of Rev. James A. Foster. There was then living at that time, at least three members of the church who were present in the organizing meeting of the convention: Deacon Thomas Miles, 422 North Union Street; Mrs. Katie Hunter, and Mrs. Eva Palmer, all of Montgomery.

He continues, relating the pastor's statement that although far removed from 1880, the church still has strong interests in foreign missions. Dr. Freeman spoke next, to Deacon Thomas Miles, a Sunday School student at the time of the organization. He was later chosen to become a teacher in the Sunday School, and built his class up to sixty students. He also served the church as custodian for a period of forty years. At the time of the interview by Dr. Freeman he was eighty five years old. The following is his testimony:

Joseph Morgan

> The Foreign Convention was organized to do Christian work, and to push the mission work. "I was present on the day the convention was organized. They opened by singing a hymn followed by a 'call to prayer.' "I do not remember who was presiding, but I do remember several persons who were present; Rev. Mansfield Taylor, Rev. James A. Foster, Rev. McAlpine, Brother Walsh Stevens, and 'Father Jenkins.' Rev. McAlpine was elected the first president."

Deacon Miles continues his account of the events of that day by
Describing what the weather was like on that occasion:

> The auditorium, including the gallery, was full. It was a mild day with a few spots of light clouds that day in November 1880. The thing that stirred interest was the fact that the Negro Baptists were about to launch forth in an organized way into the missionary enterprise to make history along with their brethren of the Christian faith. There was a big basket dinner.

The Black Baptist Church

As Deacon Miles further recalls, the missionary agents would return

To the church on speaking engagements and large sums of money would be raised for missions. When asked how he felt about the present missionary program his reply was:

> The colored Baptists should indeed support the mission work because the forefathers founded and promoted this great work. For if it had been for their interests and their sacrifices in it, it would have been done away with a long time ago. Their prayers have got things tied now! The present generation should be more loyal and give freely because this is a Christian work, and it is our duty to support it. The Commission of our Lord is just as binding upon Negro Baptists as upon other people of this world.[2]

Thus, the Foreign Mission Convention was organized as Reverend Colley gaveled the meeting to order and announced the purpose for which they were in session. In the course of the meeting, Colley was chosen as the first corresponding secretary of the convention, and Rev. W. H.

Joseph Morgan

McAlpine was elected president. Rev. Colley served as the corresponding secretary until 1883 when he gave up that office to become the convention's first missionary to Africa. The team consisted of the Reverend and Mrs. Colley, Rev. and Mrs. J. H. Presley, J. J. Coles, and H. McKinney. The team established the mission at Grand Cape Mount. Mrs. Presley's health failed and she died on the mission field, both she and her child, in less than a year. After that, the Reverend Presley was also overtaken with an illness that forced him to return to this country a helpless invalid.[3]

Guiding principles for the convention were set forth in the Preamble of its Constitution. The Executive or Foreign Mission Board was set up according to article 6 of the Constitution where its duties are clearly defined. The Board established its headquarters at Richmond, Virginia.

The controlling thought in the minds of the founders of the Foreign Mission Convention was that it would be a vehicle uniting all black Baptists in the missionary enterprise. It failed to achieve that goal for there were at least two regional conventions that did not unite with this new convention; the Baptist African Mission Convention, and the New England Convention, along with a number of smaller groups who held out.

The Reverend W. J. Simmons of Louisville, Kentucky; himself a national figure, held discussions with prominent black Baptist leaders on the matter, and at his suggestion letters were sent out announcing a call for a meeting in Saint Louis, Missouri. Six hundred delegates were in attendance at the meeting. The date was August 26, 1886, convening at the First Baptist Church of that city. The new convention chose the name "The American National Baptist Convention," and Reverend W. J. Simmons was elected president.

This is now the second major national body for Negroes of any real significance, and while it engendered some sense of pride among blacks, yet it lacked the unifying force that would bring together all the independent black organizations in a single national body. The failures in these efforts are not traceable to any singular cause. Reasons may be suggested as to what went wrong, and among them should be the possibility of placing too much responsibility upon one or two, or at most, a very few persons; lack of responsible oversight and supervision, lack of sufficient funds to adequately scrutinize the business functions, perhaps there was wrong distribution, or any number of other viable conclusions after the facts. One would hesitate to suggest embezzlement or the ciphoning off of funds for personal use by some Christian officials, but this is of a certainty, a very definite possibility.

The three major national bodies met in Montgomery, Alabama to hear reports of the work, and having received reports from several committees an earnest appeal was made for the unifying of black Baptists throughout the land. Responding to the appeal, Dr. A. W. Peques, a graduate of Bucknell University, a scholar and orator, submitted the following resolution:

Whereas, the interests and purposes of the three national bodies, namely, the Foreign Mission, the National and Educational Conventions, can be conserved and fostered under the auspices of one body; and whereas, the consolidation of the above named bodies will economize both time and money. Therefore, be it resolved, that the Foreign Convention appoint a committee of nine, who shall enter immediately into consultation with the Executive Boards of the National and Educational Conventions for the purpose of effecting a consolidation of the three bodies upon the following plan:

1. That there shall be one national organization of American Baptists.

2. Under this there shall be a Foreign Mission Board, with authority to plan and execute the foreign mission work according to the spirit and purpose set forth by the Foreign Mission Convention of the United States of America.

3. That there shall be a Board of Education and a Board of Missions to carry into effect the spirit and purpose of the National and Educational Conventions, respectively.[3]

Joseph Morgan

The resolution was accepted and the committee went to work. The next meeting was held in 1895 at Atlanta, Georgia. The body heard and discussed the actions of the committee. Their report was adopted and made a permanent part of the record. With the adoption of the new Constitution together with the Preamble setting forth the spirit and purpose of the body, the National Baptist Convention of the United States of America came into existence. The next important function to be undertaken was the selection of officers, and the establishment of the auxiliaries through which the convention was to carry on its work. The Reverend E. C. Morris was chosen as the first president of the convention. The founding date of record is given as September 28, 1895.

The convention then selected three new boards; The Foreign Mission Board, Rev. J. H. Frank, Chairman; Daniel A. Caddie, Treasurer; William H. Steward, Secretary; Dr. L. M. Luke, Corresponding Secretary. The Home Mission Board, Rev. G.W.D. Gaines, Chairman; J. A. Booker, Recording Secretary; R. H. Boyd, Corresponding Secretary. The third board was the Educational Board, the Rev. A.

Wilbanks, Chairman; W. Bishop Johnson, Corresponding Secretary.

Three months following his election to the Foreign Mission Board post, the Rev. Luke was stricken with serious illness and passed away a short time later. The successor to that post was the rev. L. G. Jordan. Soon after his selection for that post, he moved the headquarters of the Board from Richmond, Virginia to Louisville, Kentucky, and there it remained for quite some time. The move aroused resentment among the brethren in Richmond, Virginia, North Carolina, and the surrounding areas, and their support was lost to the Board and the Convention. They withdrew to form the Lott Carey Foreign Mission in Washington, D. C., in 1897. Subsequently the group returned to reunite with the convention, but did not remain, withdrawing a short time later.

The American Baptist Publication Society had been the Publishing House furnishing literature to all the Baptist Churches and organizations in the United States for a number of years. The Southern Baptist Convention was in the process of becoming self-sufficient in their own publishing

Joseph Morgan

business. A number of the brethren in the Lott Carey group were employed by the American Baptist Publication Society, and when rumors began to circulate that the National Baptists were considering the merits of establishing their own publishing house, the Society invited a number of Negro leaders and scholars to write for its "Sunday School Teacher." At this point the Southern Baptists entered a formal protest, and the invitation to Negro brethren was promptly withdrawn. That action came as a public insult to the Negro brethren, and the idea of a publishing house operated by Negroes providing literature for Negro Baptists became more appealing. Dr. E. K. Love furnished the needed incentive in a rousing address to the body, and after that, a resolution was adopted to establish a publishing board. In perspective, the major reason for the rift of the Lott Carey group arose from the fact that they were employed by the publication society as book agents promoting the sale of American Baptist Publication Society literature among black Baptists. This, added to the decision to change the headquarters of the Foreign Mission Board, proved to be too much for the Lott Carey Group. They withdrew in pursuit of their own goals, severing all connections with the National Baptist Convention.

The Black Baptist Church

Excerpts of Dr. Love's address at the Annual Session of 1896 are quoted from Dr. Freeman's work, The Epoch of the Negro Baptists And The Foreign Mission Board.

> As closely connected and as affectionately attached to the American Baptist Publication Society as I am, I could not be so disloyal as to rebel against my race and denomination after the National Baptist head decided by vote to establish a national Baptist Publishing House. I am a loyal Baptist and a loyal Negro. I still stand or fall, live or die, with my race and denomination; where they die I will die and there will I be buried. There is as strong an argument for a Negro Baptist Publishing House as there is for Negro churches, schools or families. There is not as bright and glorious a future before a Negro in a white institution as there is for him in his own . . . A people who man no enterprises show that they have no spirit of progress; and a people without this cannot command the recognition of nations and the respect of the world . . . As a people's literature is, so are they.[4]

Joseph Morgan

The Publishing Board, whose creation was a prime factor in the defection of the Lott Carey group, was also to become the center of an even more serious breach, which finally came to a head in 1915. The great haste associated with the establishing of the Publishing Board left loose ends untied, and led to the choice of the wrong personality under which the publishing concern was to function. The Publishing Board was established at the second annual meeting of the National Baptist Convention, and responsibility for its operation was assigned to the Home Missions Board. Rev. R. H. Boyd was corresponding secretary of the Board, and was known for his business acumen. It may be said that Boyd wore a 'two story hat,' in that while he was corresponding secretary of the Home Missions Board, he also became corresponding secretary of the Publishing Board. He saw the potential for personal gain and used it to his own advantage. Accomplishing his ends at the expense of the convention, he moved the headquarters of the Boards to Nashville, Tennessee, and incorporated the Publishing Board under his own name independent of the National Baptist Convention as the National Baptist Publishing Board, and used personnel of the Home Mission Board to circulate the literature produced

The Black Baptist Church

by the publishing house and to establish an extensive mailing list. Pelt (1960) shows that in nine years the publishing concern had done an aggregate business totaling 2.4 million dollars, so also, Dr. Freeman (1953).

During the years of struggle between Boyd and the convention, Boyd sought to subjugate the will of the convention to his own will by maintaining control of the Home Mission Board. Ensuing litigation favored Boyd's position with regard to ownership of the Publishing Board and consequent control thereof. The convention charter was revised showing the status of its boards, and directed that the books of the Publishing Board be submitted to the convention's auditor so that an accounting could be made of the Board's financial affairs. Boyd, of course, refused, pointing out that the convention had no claim, formal or otherwise, on his Tennessee corporation, and thereupon withdrew the Publishing Board from the convention and made it the nucleus of a new group, The National Baptist Convention, Unincorporated. The National Baptist Convention, USA., Inc., continued as the larger and older body, but without its publishing facility. As it began anew to establish new means of serving the

Joseph Morgan

National Baptist constituency, it set up first the legal framework within which the board would function as a publishing agent for the Convention. The resulting establishment was the Sunday School Publishing Board of the National Baptist Convention, USA., Inc.

Growing Pains

The National Baptist Convention today, is the third largest 'Protestant' denomination in the United States of America, and the largest Negro denomination in all the world.- - - Let it be noted here, that use of the term "Protestant," is not the choice of the author of this work; it is from works used in research for needed information to produce this work. It must also be observed that the Baptist faith is of Divine origin, and did not emerge from Catholicism. The Baptist faith is Scripture-based, see Matthew 3: 1 ff; Mt. 21: 25 f., et. al. At the time of Pelt's writing (1960), the Convention records showed enrollments totaling more than 27,500 ministers, and churches totaling 26,000 comprising a black Baptist constituency in excess of five million members. More recent tabulations show National Baptist Convention churches with memberships exceeding 6,500,000.

The Black Baptist Church

The Convention as it stands today, has come through many difficult periods at the price of great pain to itself. Three defections during the life of the Convention from 1895 to the present, although painful, have proved to be growing and learning experiences. The growing pains of the Convention have proven to be the birth pains of two other national bodies; The National Baptist Convention, Unincorporated, and the Progressive National Baptist Convention. The formation of the Unincorporated Convention in 1915, arising from disagreement regarding control of the National Baptist Publishing Board has been discussed above. The third convention, the second child of the National Baptist Convention, was born of a two-part constitutional question: the tenure of office which would limit the term of the president to four consecutive one-year terms, and the power to elect and direct the office of the executive secretary of the Convention by the Board of Directors. The Convention's only right in this matter would be that of approval of the selection by the Board. The final resolution of the matter was met with disapproval from some quarters, which resulted in the withdrawal from the Convention by those who had vigorously opposed the matter in which the question was settled. According to Torbet (1950, 1963), this faction, with delegates from fourteen states, met in Cincinnati November 15, 1961 and formerly withdrew from the National Baptist Convention to form the Progressive National Baptist Convention.

Black Baptist Conventions, a concept which began with the formation of the organization of the Providence Baptist Association of Ohio, which was soon followed by the organization of the Wood River Baptist Association of Illinois. The first of these came into existence in 1836, and the second, in 1839. The movement thus begun culminated in the organization of the National Baptist Convention of the United States of America, Incorporated.

The Baptist Associations, the Regional Conventions, State Conventions, and other Baptist auxiliary bodies by free association through membership representation of member-churches from what Vada P. Felder terms "A MIGHTY ARMY." These bodies form an extension of the fellowship and missionary activity of the black Baptist churches with their pastors as the first authorized delegate, or messenger of the churches.

CONCLUSION

The organization of the black Baptist church, and the role of the black Baptist Pastor, are of vital interest to every member of a black Baptist church. The concluding portion of this work brings into focus the pastor's role as under shepherd, teacher and interpreter of the Word of God to the people of his congregation, as preacher, prophet, and minister of Christ to His church.

Dubois, in his "Souls of Black Folk," has appraised the Negro preacher as what remained of the West African Priest or Medicine-man. He made his appearance on the plantation early as a spiritual/judicial 'handy-man.' Under the guise of bard, doctor, judge, and priest within the limits of slavery, the Negro preacher emerges as healer of the sick, interpreter of the Unknown, comforter of the sorrowing, and supernatural avenger of wrong. The Negro preacher, however he is derived, was before the Negro church, and the black church, the first Afro-American institution, arose under the black preacher. So that it may be rightly said that as the preacher was, so the church became.

Joseph Morgan

At the time of Dubois' writing, the church was deemed the social center of the Negro's life in America. The truth of this lies in the fact that legislation did not favor free access to social, cultural, or economic development for the Negro. And, thus, the Negro's whole life centered around the black church. What educational opportunities were granted to him found its first expression in the church. He became orator, parliamentarian, and politician through the only outlet open to him; the black church. Dubois' estimation of the black church is hardly more than belittling, yet it must be observed that the black church, Baptist in particular, has had considerable impact upon this nation for good in both the political arena and the Christian community.

The organizational structure of the institutional black Baptist church consists of auxiliaries, boards, and committees. Membership development through Christian education and training in the duties of church membership are accomplished through the Sunday School and the Baptist Training Union. The church program of evangelism is carried on through the Sunday School as well as through visitation evangelism. Methods vary according to congregation and pastor. With some churches there is a spring revival, and another in the fall, while still others would promote an annual two-week evangelistic service. With some, the Sunday evening hour is the evangelistic hour, and Bible study apart from the Sunday School, is for the mid-week worship services.

The Music Department of the black Baptist church, is structured according to the needs of a particular church program, as set up by the Minister of Music in cooperation with the pastor of the church. Other auxiliaries of the church are the Usher Group and Nurse Unit (First Aid). Women's Missionary Society, which has a weekly mission study group meeting, sometimes, at the church building, and at specified times, the meeting may be held at Convalescent Homes or Nursing Homes.

The Deaconship and the Trustees have varying functions at different local situations, but primarily, the Deacons serve at the tables and have charge of receipt and disposition of church funds, and are charged with seeing to the general welfare of the pastor and the church building, and other properties of the church. They also assist the pastor in administering the ordinances of the church, and such other duties as the pastor may assign.

In some states churches holding property are required by state law to have trustees, in which cases, the trustees become custodians of the churches' legal documents, sign contracts for the church and ascertain that all the financial obligations of the church are kept current. Trustees are also custodians of the churches' funds, and are the banking committees responsible for all disbursements. There is no set pattern for all churches, and circumstances will alter cases in each local situation.

The church staff in a large number of black churches are volunteer workers, with the possible exception of the church clerk. Some of the larger churches would perhaps employ a part-time staff, or a full time secretary and custodian according to church needs.

Funding in the black Baptist church, especially the

The Black Baptist Church

church with the smaller membership, is through the Sunday offerings. Where tithing and free-will liberal giving is taught, some of the membership become tithers, and a few are liberal givers, that is they give an amount above what their tithe should be on a regular basis. The faithful members, those holding the church as dear to their hearts, when absent from the fellowship, will mail their contribution to the church in their regular offering envelopes. Some churches operate on a system of pledges; each member is required to pledge a certain amount for the year.

The present interest in the black church and its perspective is not new. Rather it proves to be renewed interest. Many voices have spoken, observations have been made, and studies have been done for just about every facet of the black man's existence, here and elsewhere. Writers have varying concepts of the black man's perspective on life, and his world views. There are reasons for this: no one, black or white, can speak for the race as a whole. No special personality commands the respect and allegiance of the black race. It must be that the black man is first of all a person, then a human being; he is an individual whose perspective is very

Joseph Morgan
likely to be colored by his experience.

The same is held to be true of the black church. While there is much talk about segregation within the churches during the 11 o'clock hour on Sunday morning, it must be remembered that if there is segregation in the churches it is not restricted to race. People tend to group themselves off according to their several experiences and life situations. The theological perspective of the black preacher and the black church has much to do with the life experiences that touch their being on a daily basis. Background helps to shape one's personality and make one what one is.

Studies were made of the civil rights struggles and the riots of the 1950's and 1960's, the general unrest throughout the nation, and the violent deaths of the Kennedys; John F., and Robert, and the death by asassination, of Dr. Martin Luther King, Jr. It was feared that much of the black community would become a seething, armed camp looking for revenge. Fear settled among many people, black and white, and unfounded suspicion became the order of the day. Riding the

The Black Baptist Church

crest of the wave of fear, James Forman sought to capitalize on the situation with his "Black Manifesto," with which he began a series of confrontations of the white churches in Detroit and New York, and the trend began to spread far and wide. What he started degenerated into the lowliest kind of evil, for others took up the mantle, and under the guise of the "struggle for black rights," began to intimidate churches at worship, forcing their way in and walking down the aisles enmasse to make demands of the church establishment. The point to which the movement degenerated may be observed in the actions of the few who defiled the Lord's Table by spitting in the communion cups and defecating in the aisles of some of the churches. The whole movement began to break down when black pastors and church congregations openly condemned the whole movement. Smear campaigns were conducted against many pastors in the Saint Louis black community because they refused to go along with the tide of events. Church members supported their ministers, rising up in indignation at the thought of anyone who would dare to defile any church. Thus it withered away and died, at least for the time being.

Joseph Morgan

The foregoing general picture of how people tend to react to crisis situations should provide some idea of the relationship between the black pastor and his charge; his pastorate. How the church responds to the pastor is largely determined by the pastor himself. The study of the black Baptist church has provided the writer with some new insights that were not readily apparent before. The black Baptist church came into existence when slavery was the law of the land. Although it owes its inception as an institutional church to the devoted labors of white Baptist missionaries, it is not 'white Baptist' oriented. The tension that manifests itself between black and white Baptists has often arisen from the fact that many of the white churches and pastors not only condoned the system of slavery, but thrived on it. Many blacks are sensitive on that issue, and have some difficulty dealing with it. Just here, the black pastor has accomplished a monumental task in teaching his people the Biblical concepts of forgiveness, and the growth in Christlike-ness engendered thereby. Perhaps one of the most difficult tasks the black preacher had to assume, was that, of teaching his people not to hate. His great success as a black leader is owed to the fact that he has shared their experiences, and

The Black Baptist Church was one among them. He knew their longings, and the deep desires of their hearts, and was able, on the basis of his own background and needs, to speak to their needs.

Chapter 7

NOTES

1. David and Alberta Shipley, <u>History of Black Baptists in Missouri,</u> Missionary Baptist State Convention of Missouri, Dr. I. H. Henderson, Jr., President n.p., n.d., pp. 52 – 55.
2. Edward A. Freeman, op. cit., pp. 70 – 71.
3. Ibid. p. 81
4. Ibid. pp. 89 – 90.

BIBLIOGRAPHY

RESOURCES ON METHODOLOGY, FORM AND STYLE   Campbell, William Giles, and Ballou, Stephen Vaughn, <u>Form and Style</u>
<u>Theses, Reports, Term Papers,</u> Fourth Edition, Boston; Houghton
Mifflin Company, 1974.

Owens, B. Lezelle, (Author), <u>A Guide for Writers.</u>

RESOURCES ON SUBJECT MATTER

Bergman, Peter M., <u>The Chronological History of the Negro in America,</u>
New York; Harper & Row Publishers, 1969.

Bragdon, Henry W., and McCutchen, Samuel P. <u>History of a Free People,</u>
New York; The Macmillan Company, 1967.

Day, Richard Ellsworth, <u>Rhapsody in Black, The Life Story of John Jasper,</u>
Valley Forge, Pa.; The Judson Press, 1953.

Franklin, John Hope, <u>From Slavery to Freedom, A History of Negro</u>
<u>Americans,</u> New York; Vintage Books, A Division

of Random House, 1967.

Frazier, E. Franklin, <u>The Negro Church in America,</u> New York, Schocken

Books, 1974.

Freeman, E. A., <u>The Epoch of the Negro Baptists and the Foreign Mission</u>

<u>Board,</u> National Baptist Convention, USA., Inc., Kansas City, Kansas; The Central Seminary Press, 1953.

Greene, Lorenzo J., Kremer, Gary R., and Holland, Anthony F., <u>Missouri's</u>

<u>Black Heritage,</u> Saint Louis, Missouri; Forum Press, 1980.

Katz, William Loren, <u>Eyewitness: The Negro in American History,</u> New

York; Pitman Publishing Company, 1967.

Murch, James DeForest, <u>Christian Education and the Local Church,</u> Revised

Edition, 1958, Cincinnati; Standard Publishing Company, 1943.

Pelt, Owen D., and Smith, Ralph Lee, <u>The Story of the National Baptists,</u>

New York; Vantage Press, 1960.

Rawick, George P., From Sundown to Sunup; The Making of the Black Community, Connecticut; Greenwood Publishing Company, 1972.

Shipley, David and Alberta, History of Black Baptists in Missouri, Missionary Baptist State Convention of Missouri, n.p., n.d.

REFERENCES

Dubois, W. E. B., from <u>Three Negro Classics,</u> New York; Avon Books,
1965, 338 - 345

Felder, Vada P., <u>A Mighty Army,</u> National Baptist Training Union Board,
Nashville, Tennessee; n.d.

Ginsburg, Ralph, <u>100 Years of Lynchings,</u> New York ; Lancer Books, 1969.

Jackson, J. H., <u>A Story of Christian Activism,</u> The History of the National
Baptist Convention, USA., Inc., Nashville, Tnn.; Townsend Press,
1980, 406 – 495

Johnson, James Weldon, and J. Rosamond, <u>The Books of American Negro
Spirituals,</u> New York; The Viking Press, 1969, Introduction.

Jordan, L. G., <u>The Baptist Standard Church Directory, and Busy Pastor's
Guide,</u> Nashville, Tnn., Sunday School Publishing Board, NBC,

USA. Inc. 1929. 37 – 55, Cf. Hiscox, Edward T., "The Hiscox Guide

For Baptist Churches," wherein see "Baptist Confessions." See further

Pendleton, J. M., Baptist Church Manual" "Doctrines of a Baptist Church." See also J. G. Bow, What Baptists Believe and Why They

Believe it

Shipley, David and Alberta, History of Black Baptists in Missouri, The

Missionary Baptist State Convention of Missouri, Dr. I. H. Henderson, Jr., President, n.p., n.d.

Torbet, Robert G., A History of Baptists, Valley Forge; The Judson Press,

1950, 353 – 355, 477.

Washington, Booker T., from Three Negro Classics, New York; Avon

Books, 1965, 41 – 49.

Wilmore, Gayraud S., and Cone, James H., Black Theology; A

Documentary History, 1966 – 1979, Maryknoll, New York; Orbis Books, 1979, 80 – 89.

PERIODICAL

Review and Expositor, A Baptist Theological Journal, Published by the
   Faculty of the Southern Baptist Theological Seminary, Louisville, Ky.
   Volume LXX, No. 3, Summer, 1973, 295 – 300.

Printed in the United States
16646LVS00002B/85-126